Baseball
ROAD TRIPS

THE MIDWEST AND GREAT LAKES

TIMOTHY M. MULLIN

Library of Congress Cataloging-in-Publication Data has been applied for.

This book is available in quantity at special discounts for your group or organization. For further information, contact:

Triumph Books LLC
814 North Franklin Street
Chicago, Illinois 60610
(312) 337-0747
www.triumphbooks.com

Printed in U.S.A.
ISBN: 978-1-60078-969-4
Design by Andy Hansen
Icons and "Baseball Road Trip" logo design by Karen Schmidt

CONTENTS

• •

INTRODUCTION

Bear with me travelistas. I have to provide a half-hearted (and likely, half-witted) history lesson.

The heartland of the United States is where baseball found its professional footing after the end of the American Civil War. As peace and the Reconstruction settled in, interest in baseball grew. The industrial East Coast was working to recover its industrial footing and the South was struggling back from the Civil War.

The Midwest was relatively unscathed. Emerging cities like Chicago, Cincinnati, Indianapolis, Louisville, and St. Louis were becoming major whistle-stops on an expanding national rail map with ambitions of reaching the Pacific before 1870. Peace was taking hold and economically there was nowhere else but up. Where there is peace and economic growth, entertainment follows. Baseball came along at the right time in American history.

Professional baseball players in the shadow of the Civil War were only professional in the sense that they were paid hired guns who rambled about the countryside with rag-tag teams. Many were quality ballplayers. Many were rogues who fixed games. The questionable reputation the game was developing concerned the ethical ballplayers. These gentlemen wanted a unified set of professional rules of the game that incorporated guidelines that prevented wagering and rooted out ne'er-do-wells.

As this general movement developed, the first professional baseball organization was the Cincinnati Red Stockings (now the Reds), formed in 1869. The full formation of rules and guidelines became a reality in New York City on March 17, 1871, with the formal recognition of the National Association of Professional Base Ball Players (the National Association). "Gentleman clubs" otherwise known as baseball organizations popped up from Boston to St. Louis. Where the rail lines went, so did professional baseball.

Boston, New York City, and Troy (New York), were the locales of the first professional baseball organizations on the Eastern Seaboard. However, the first teams and cities in professional baseball were decidedly Midwestern. The Chicago White Stockings, Cleveland Forest Cities, Fort Wayne Kekiongas, Rockford Forest Cities, and Cincinnati Red Stockings offered this wide-open sport to cities and towns that had room for expansion. The Midwest was verdant country for opportunity at the time. Baseball was a hopeful game being embraced by a hopeful country. For the next four seasons, the basis for a stronger model for professional baseball was being developed. You guessed it: the league expanded too fast, franchise instability ruled, the money got bigger, and owners wanted more control over the players.

Only three teams survived the folding of the National Association era. On February 2, 1876, the National League was formed. The Midwest was represented well among the first franchises entered into the National League. The Chicago White Stockings, Cincinnati Red Stockings, Louisville Grays, and St. Louis Brown Stockings were among the charter members of the new league. Over the next 40 years, professional baseball would evolve into the business we know today as Major League Baseball. A two-league, multi-division organization of rules and guidelines meant to provide stability and root out the scoundrels.

See…I told you it would be as cursory a lesson as you can get.

I'm not a historian. I'm a baseball travel writer. However, I wanted to give you the above basis in history. I wanted to emphasize the importance of the Great Lakes and Midwest in baseball's development. Baseball's expansion parallels this country's expansion. As immigrants and established business leaders moved westward to seek opportunity, baseball came along and entertained these people.

Wherever there were wide-open fields of green grass, baseball was played there. In the 1850s and 1860s, open fields were the fodder of dreams for big-city dwellers. The Civil War and its subsequent end exposed millions of Bostonians, New Yorkers, and Chicagoans to the Midwest and South. Many stayed. Many were soon to come back in large part due to the wide-open spaces. These people built the second slice of America that soon opened the door to the embryonic western United States.

Midwestern professional baseball at the major and minor league level has maintained a reverence for its history. Century-old stadiums like Wrigley Field (Chicago) or Modern Woodmen Ballpark (Davenport/Quad Cities) offer fans a touchstone with the past. New ballparks like Target Field in Minneapolis or Louisville Slugger Field compliment the past in their design and stay respectful to the design from Midwestern baseball's earliest days. Apart from the 1970s-prototypical spaceship stadiums in Cincinnati and St. Louis, cities and towns throughout the Midwest have committed themselves to the concept of ballpark as architectural landmark.

Now more than ever, baseball fans can affordably plan three-, five-, and seven-day trips through the Midwest and around the Great Lakes. Major airlines like Southwest and American service all state capitals in the Midwest and the major cities that dot the Great Lakes. In some cases, you can affordably fly into mid-sized cities that rule the map in this wonderful area of the country.

The dream can be achieved. State tourism authorities are working with cities and towns to target the professional baseball traveler as one worthy of hotel and rental car specials. Every state in the Great Lakes has a distinct baseball history, and trips can be affordably planned to experience that history. Any determined fan with a dream and access to the Internet can set up the trip of their dreams—even a trip that includes a visit to the Field of Dreams in Dyersville, Iowa.

My recommendations throughout this book will focus on the individual ballparks, cities, and towns on their own. As well, suggestions for planned trips within certain states and areas are provided. From a long weekend in Cleveland to experience the city and "the Jake" to a seven-day jaunt from Minneapolis to the Field of Dreams in Dyersville to Iowa City to Chicago, the dream is affordably within reach.

Another suggestion is to consider the unusual. Plan a trip on Amtrak with Cardinals fans migrating toward Wrigley Field and Chicago en masse. If you live anywhere in the U.S. and have airline miles you have difficulty using, find one-way flights to Chicago, Indianapolis, St. Louis, and back home over a five-day period. You can see the White Sox on Thursday afternoon, the Cubs on Friday afternoon, lovely Victory Field in Indy on Saturday night, get a look at the new Busch Stadium in St. Louis on Sunday, and you are back home on Monday night. All told, you will expend 50,000 airline miles. Shake it up and find a reason to travel in a different way. It may be the only way to get rid of those airline miles these days.

What I am trying to impart to you is the concept of *Explorus Maximus*: make the most of your curiosity. Explore to the maximum level. I am one of those people who see hitting Dick and Joan's 220 Supper Club after a Wisconsin Timber Rattlers game as just as exciting as a steak at Gibson's after a Chicago Cubs game. Why? *Explorus Maximus*. Meet new people, experience new things, and have new adventures.

The Midwest offers the baseball traveler literally hundreds of opportunities to meet new people, see new things, and go off the beaten path. From the Iron Range of Minnesota to the coal mines of Kentucky, you can find quality accommodations at an affordable price. There are thousands of great restaurants from the shores of Cleveland's Lake Erie to the farmlands of Iowa. Best of all, great major and regional airlines in the Midwest make it easier for baseball travelers to experience so many great baseball cities, towns, and shrines throughout the Midwest. The wide-open spaces dotted with cities of great opportunity accented with towns of uncontested decency.

Poet Carl Sandburg was a son of the Midwest. One of my favorite quotes from the Prairie bard is, "There is an eagle in me that wants to soar, and there is a hippopotamus in me that wants to wallow in the mud." Travel the Midwest and hit enough of its great cities and towns, and you will understand, too. Your drive from town to city to town will be set apart by cornfields that show off sunsets as beautiful as any given to you by any ocean. The Great Lakes are not as much lakes as mammoth mini-oceans with unique characteristics and a different temperament.

Our third coast and its adjacent countryside rival the ocean/inland beauty of New England or the California coast. A summertime drive on the Circle/Red Arrow Highway around Lake Michigan is among America's underrated driving treasures. You can plan your travel to go for the whole enchilada (which takes days) or achieve a two- to three-day trip with the help of the Great Lakes car ferry (www.ssbadger.com) that connects Manitowoc, Wisconsin, with Ludington, Michigan. Either way, you can see a lot of beauty and a lot of great baseball.

Along that ride, you can take in baseball at all levels and enjoy cities and towns that welcome you with the typical open arms that Midwesterners provide. "Welcome," "Where are you from?" and "What do you plan on doing on your stay?" will be asked by many and with complete sincerity by all wherever you drive in the Midwest. My friends from outside of the Midwest ask me about "Midwest nice." There's no real mystery to "Midwest nice." It is what it is. We Midwesterners aren't offended that people are reticent to accept the kindness. We just know nice is a great place to start a relationship. Things will grow from there.

Baseball fans traveling the Midwest will have no shortage of options to consider in their planning. To start out small, you could check out the little-known Northwoods League. The Northwoods League rivals its older brother the Cape Cod League for college talent with big-league potential. A schedule of 56 games is played by 15 teams in small to mid-sized towns in Iowa, Minnesota, and Wisconsin. In the movie *Field of Dreams*, Ray Kinsella refers to the experience of a young Archibald "Moonlight" Graham playing in small towns around the Midwest to keep his dream alive. The towns of the Northwoods League are those towns: small hamlets that provide shelter and a livable wage at a local company to a college ballplayer wanting to keep fresh during their summer away from school.

A section later in the book focuses on the success story of the Madison Mallards of the Northwoods League. Tips are given regarding notable hotels, accommodations, and attractions in many of the towns of the Northwoods League, as well. Fans can get more information about this hidden jewel of the upper Midwest at www.northwoodsleague.com.

Fans looking for an even grittier level of semi-pro baseball can look into the independent league in the Midwest known as the Frontier League. Teams in independent leagues are not affiliated with Major League Baseball clubs or an affiliated minor league team. These teams exist without the consent of Major League Baseball, as well. The Frontier League does, however, have rules and guidelines much like the major and minor league system.

Hired guns unwanted by big league teams trying to find new life at the end of their career can make a maximum of $72,000 playing for a Frontier League team. You also have young players earning $600 a month trying to get noticed by a scout who may have the ear of an MLB team. Many of these players suffered injuries in college or the minor leagues and were discarded when rosters were settled at all levels of a major league organization. The players of the Frontier League play as hard as players at any level of baseball.

A few of the Frontier League's players have scrapped their way to the major leagues since the league's inception in 1993. Many of the teams in the Frontier League are located in and around larger cities like Chicago, Pittsburgh, Cleveland, and St. Louis. The Frontier League schedules 100 games a year.

A side chapter in the book is dedicated to a few side trips on which baseball fans can attempt to catch a Frontier League game. I recommend a few places to eat in this book. One place I am featuring is in a Frontier League town: Wolf's Barbeque in Evansville, Indiana. If I have the bad fortune to end up on Death Row, Wolf's Barbeque will be on my wish list for a last meal. For now, I will keep my nose clean, deal on the up and up, and grab lunch at Wolf's before I hit an Evansville Otters game. For more information, check out www.frontierleague.com.

You will have no shortage of quality affiliated minor league experiences in the Midwest League. The Midwest League has 16 solid organizations in Illinois, Indiana, Iowa, Kentucky, Michigan, Ohio, and Wisconsin. Many sections of the book are dedicated to the classically beautiful ballparks in this league that has been around since 1954 (since 1947 if you include its time as the Illinois State D League). The cities and towns of the Midwest League are quaint. This quaintness makes for great getaways for couples and families throughout the Midwest. These are the cities and towns most likely to offer you a bed and breakfast, a four-star dinner, and a classic ballpark in the Midwest.

St. Louis, Chicago, Detroit, and Milwaukee may be bigger and offer big-city amenities, but baseball travelers can run into some great deals in some beautiful towns in the Midwest League.

The leagues themselves offer a lot of great road-trip opportunities. However, fans can plan a road trip within each state and see multiple levels of baseball. Each state in the Midwest has unique offerings for baseball and ballpark fans.

For instance, Cleveland Indians fans can scout a good chunk of their minor and major league talent within five days and without leaving the state of Ohio. The trip can start in Columbus, where the Indians AAA affiliate Columbus Clippers play in gorgeous Huntington Park. Stay a night and enjoy Columbus, then dash up I-71 and over on I-77 to visit Canal Park at Main and Exchange Streets in downtown Akron. Akron's Canal Park is one of the best baseball experiences for fans who want to keep score, hear the quiet, and enjoy an Akron Aeros (AA/Eastern League) ballgame. The radio call and atmosphere at Canal Park is a blissful throwback to another era.

You would then take a dash to the east side of Cleveland to see the Lake County Captains, the Midwest League (A) affiliate of the Cleveland Indians. The Captains play at Classic Park and often have afternoon games. Time it right and you can see the youngest talent play at Classic Park in the afternoon and the Cleveland Indians at Progressive Field in the evening.

Later in the book, a five- to seven-day venture through Iowa is featured. In Minnesota, you can experience the organic feel of multiple towns with small ballparks in the Northwoods League before ending up at the wonder that is Target Field. Kentucky's Bourbon Trail falls in line with beautiful ballparks in Bowling Green, Lexington, and Louisville. Indiana's ballparks in Indianapolis and across the northern tier of the state make for a great buildup to Chicago's U.S. Cellular Field and Wrigley Field. Michigan is a multi-city, multi-league adventure that takes you from Detroit to Grand Rapids with great small towns, beach towns, and coastline to enjoy. You can see a 200-pound duck fly in Madison, Wisconsin (we'll explain later), and meet the kindest rattlesnake in the world, Fang, at Appleton's Time Warner Field.

The Midwest is full of great options for ballpark and baseball lovers. With the Internet, planning is easier than ever to make the most of a three-, five-, or seven-day trip through the Midwest. Even a one-day getaway can be best planned with the help of this guide. It is all about making the most of the time you are given to affordably enjoy yourself.

A lot of great people traversed from Europe and the East Coast and settled in the Midwest. Baseball came with them and it is part of the great history of this great area of the country. Chart a course as these pioneers, settlers, and immigrants once did and appreciate the historic and unique baseball parks of the Midwest. Let your mind wander, plan wisely, and let the American pastime be a part of your American leisure.

Oh, and one more thing…*Exploris Maximus*. Enjoy.

CHAPTER 1

ILLINOIS

· ·

North Side, South Side, and the Countryside

WRIGLEY FIELD
Home of the Chicago Cubs

• •

1060 West Addison St., Chicago, IL, 60613
(773) 404-2827 / www.cubs.mlb.com / Another good web source in the area is
www.lakeviewchamber.com if you are looking for information on businesses in
and around Lakeview/Wrigleyville. For information on other areas of Chicago,
try looking at www.tourismchicago.org.

In 1914, eventual Chicago Cubs co-owner Charlie Weeghman built
Weeghman Park to house his then–Federal League team, the Chicago
Federals (aka the Chicago Whales). The Whales and the Federal
League went the way of the dodo and folded in late 1916. This left
Weeghman with a partially completed $250,000 ballpark on his hands
and no tenant.

In true Chicago fashion, where a vacuum exists a deal soon will take
place to fill it. Weeghman put together a consortium of investors
that included William Wrigley of chewing-gum fame and purchased
the Chicago Cubs of the National League. The Cubs played at West
Side Grounds and were more than happy to move to the shiny new
ballpark built by Weeghman on a plot of land at the corner of Clark
and Addison Streets. After all, West Side Grounds gave birth to the
idiom "out of left field"—a reference to the Cook County Hospital's
sanitarium beyond left field of West Side Grounds.

West Side Grounds was also home to the burgeoning championship
machine known as the Chicago Cubs. Between 1906 and 1910, the
Cubs were perennial challengers for the World Series, with back-
to-back success in 1907 and 1908 (yes, the Cubs were the first
back-to-back winner of the World Series). Rather than reinvest in a
dynasty, Cubs owner Charles Murphy took profits and let the grounds
go into disrepair. The vaunted Cubs became "Murphy's Spuds"
to the local media and the Cubs were cursed with the continuous
mismanagement of Murphy. Weeghman, Wrigley, and the rest of the
new owners couldn't have come along at a better time for Cubs fans.

SIDE TRIP: A VISIT TO FIRE STATION 78 ON WAVELAND AVE. IS A MUST FOR FANS

When you visit Wrigley Field, you will be inundated by every three-card huckster and timeshare sales hack trying to get your name and address with the promise of a free vacation. Avoid them and make a beeline to Fire Station 78 at 1052 West Waveland Avenue.

The men and women of Fire Station 78 will welcome you and your family to the station with open arms. The firefighters won't try to sell you on it, but the station does offer unique t-shirts on game days paying homage to their history in service to Wrigleyville. The station is very supportive of Chicago Fire Department charities through the sale of their t-shirts.

Kids love the company dog and you will grab a souvenir that helps charity and isn't run of the mill for a visit to Wrigley Field.

In 1918, William Wrigley bought out Weeghman and the other investors in the Cubs ownership. Wrigley felt as if he were the man to bring the Cubs back to the glory of the early part of the twentieth century. By 1920, the ballpark was renamed Cubs Park. On Opening Day of 1926, Cubs Park was renamed Wrigley Field. Just before the first pitch, William Wrigley signed the title documents on a cursed piece of land at home plate and the ghosts of every dead Cubs player in history poured out of nearby Graceland Cemetery and into the ballpark. Priests were performing exorcisms on the fans unfortunate enough to get caught up in the maelstrom, and the Cubs haven't won a World Series since.

All kidding aside, no team is more vexed by a curse or curses in all professional sports. Believe in curses or not, the crutch of long-standing curses add to the flavor of Wrigley Field and will make you marvel at the loyalty of Cubs fans when you get to the ballpark. Visiting Wrigley Field is akin to visiting the packed church of a religion whose tenets were all disproven by science and logic. You will still find the faithful in the grandstands and bleachers of Wrigley Field because there is always next year.

Not much has changed at Wrigley Field since Mr. Wrigley took over the note and name of the ballpark in 1926. The bleachers and classic scoreboard were built in 1937. The first home run hit by an opposing player was thrown back on the field 15 minutes later (all kidding aside, that didn't become a "tradition" until the late 20th century). Truth be told, the Wrigley Field we know today as a tough ticket wasn't a very tough ticket from 1926 to 1983. The teaser years of 1932, 1938, 1945, and 1969 drew more fans to Wrigley Field. However, empty seats were the rule rather than the exception at Wrigley Field in the Wrigley ownership era.

Then Lee Elia had his classic unexpurgated rant in 1983 and there was the National League East championship in 1984. Things suddenly

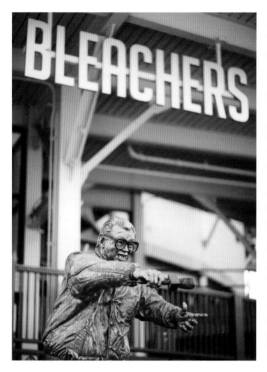

changed at Wrigley Field. The new ownership of the *Chicago Tribune* was trying to get into the curse-killing business and do the impossible: bring a World Series trophy to Wrigley Field. The *Tribune* ownership may not have succeeded on that front, but they did succeed in making Wrigley Field a marketable destination through a savvy media plan that included a cable superstation that grew their fan base exponentially.

The lights were turned on at Wrigley Field on August 8, 1988, after almost 5,700 games without them. The world didn't end, but it did rain that night and those who clung to curses took solace in what they believed was God making a loud statement.

Then you had Bartman, a blown 2003 National League Championship Series, and even the least superstitious within Cubs faithful considered the validity of the curses they ritually scoffed.

Fast forward to today. No, the Cubs still have not won a World Series since 1908. The crosstown White Sox won a World Series in 2005, ending their dry spell with destiny eight miles south of Wrigley Field. Even the Boston Red Sox won three World Series (2004, 2007, and 2013) to get off the schneide.

Wrigley Field is going through a renovation plan that includes a rebuild of how the neighborhood integrates into the Cubs "brand." The word "brand" comes off as Orwellian corporate speak, but it is applicable in this case. This renovation plan depends on Wrigley's influence on a hotel project that will replace a number of bars and the McDonald's on Clark Street.

The updates will displace the once-popular drinking dens known as the "rooftops" (the buildings beyond the left-field wall on Waveland Avenue and Sheffield Avenue). A 5,700-square-foot scoreboard will be built above the left-field bleachers, blocking the view once used by rooftop dwellers. Fans get the sense that the new ownership (the Ricketts family) is working as hard as possible to separate the drunken revelry that once ruled "Wrigleyville" from a new movement toward a family-friendly environment.

As I write this, I imagine a group of Bleacher Bums saying "Yeah, right! Good luck!" and envision my younger self meeting buddies at Guthrie's Bar on Addison at 2:00 PM for a 7:00 PM game. Making Wrigley Field more family friendly would require a fully loaded B-52 bomber strafing a six-block square area south of Wrigley Field. The largest concentration of bars near a ballpark has to be in that area of the world. Don't believe me? Go ahead, do a Google search for restaurants and bars near Wrigley Field and get ready to see a million red pins pop up.

There is still a lot of construction to go, but trying to stem off or abate the alcoholically induced joviality of the Bleacher Bums is a tall order. You can increase ticket prices, increase beer prices, and cut off beer sales earlier and earlier—it does not matter. Bleacher Bums and/or inebriated Cubs fans will always find a way to afford a ticket, afford the beer, and leave just after beer sales have ended. It's an unfortunate by-product of the massive expansion of Cubs fans in the post-WGN superstation era combined with the easy availability of Chicago liquor licenses in the ward during the 1980s.

Don't get me wrong: families can enjoy Wrigley Field. There are dedicated sections in the ballpark expressly set aside for families. These areas are few and far in between, though. Tickets for Cubs games usually go on sale for individual games just before spring training. The smart and the quick parent should plot out where the family sections are at Wrigley Field and squat on the seats they want the day Cubs tickets go on sale. These tickets tend to go quickly, so be the early bird.

The irresistible charm of Wrigley Field is worth a visit on an off day, as well. Plan well and you might be able to latch on to a planned tour of the ballpark given by the Cubs staff on non-game days. A perfect plan may be to get into Chicago a day or two before the homestand you have tickets to attend and go on the tour. The abundance of activities in the neighborhood, even on an off day, makes Wrigleyville one of baseball's special places to visit year-round.

If Wrigley Field is fun on an off day, imagine how fun it is on a game day.

Despite the lack of trophies, Wrigley Field does have its history for fans to appreciate. On May 2, 1917, fate handed the ball to Cubs starter Jim "Hippo" Vaughan and Cincinnati Reds starter Fred Toney. Both starters threw no-hitters for nine innings before legendary Olympian and Reds player Jim Thorpe drove in the winning run after a few Reds hits in the 10th inning. Toney completed the no-hitter in the 10th but the die had been cast: two starters took no-hitters beyond the regulation nine innings, amazing the fans who had gathered that day at what was a brand-new ballpark.

Babe Ruth called his shot (or didn't, depending on who you talk to) in the 1932 World Series. In 1938, you had Gabby Hartnett's homer in the dark against the Pittsburgh Pirates. Mr. Cub, Ernie Banks, graced the field through his Hall of Fame career and hit his legendary 500th home run in 1970. The controversial and legendary Pete Rose got his 4,191st hit off of the Cubs' Reggie Patterson in 1985. There are definitely more than enough ghosts for fans to feel as they walk around the steel and cement structure called Wrigley Field.

When you get inside of Wrigley Field, look at the details. Namely, look at the signs. My favorite sign at each entryway to the grandstands features the message "Be Alert for Foul Balls" with a small cartoon cub chasing down a flying baseball. This simple white-on-stadium-green sign has always said to me that Wrigley Field was meant for families and family fun. Wrigley Field has earned the moniker "World's Largest Beer Garden" from fan and foe alike. If Wrigley Field is a beer garden, the seventh-inning stretch is the rowdiest last call in America.

It would be a bold understatement to say the seventh-inning stretch at Wrigley Field is "kind of special." Expect a celebrity or athlete of note to lead the crowd for "Take Me Out to the Ball Game." This tradition, of course, was done every game by Harry Caray when he was an announcer in the Cubs radio and television booth. The management made the seventh-inning ritual a permanent fixture at Wrigley Field after his death in February 1998. Be wary of fans who have imbibed a few too many adult refreshments swaying arm to arm with friends at this time: spilled beer is a common occurrence during the seventh-inning stretch at Wrigley Field.

The food at Wrigley Field is basic baseball food. Walking the lower concourse and checking out the menu at concession stands at

Wrigley Field is an exercise in repetition: hot dogs, pizza, nachos…hot dogs, pizza, nachos. Wrigley Field doesn't need to create the unique offering. The tight, limited confines might be a reason for the menu's limitation. The management likely knows refrigeration space is limited and that determines the fan's options with older facilities.

Beer sales at Wrigley Field are among the highest per fan in baseball. The late announcer Harry Caray and the Tribune Company ushered in Anheuser-Busch beer products in the early 1980s. Chicago Cubs fans became loyal to Old Style beer in the decades previous to the change and fans resisted the change by demanding Old Style. In time, Old Style was pushed out to the margins of the ballpark by the presence of the mega-brewer. Old Style is still served at Wrigley Field for now, but it will be a sad day when it goes the way of monopoly. For the more refined tongue, you might even be able to find a foreign beer or American craft beer if you look hard enough.

The Captain Morgan Club is a bar outside of the ballpark in the right-field plaza where the Harry Caray statue stands. A full menu of food is offered (burgers, salads, pizza, etc.) and the bar selections are limitless. Premium cocktails and specialty beers are on tap. Room is limited: the fire marshal keeps it to a crowd of 600 maximum in the space.

There is no shortage of history, fun, food, and drink around Wrigley Field. Take time to get a feel for the unique relationship that the stadium has with the Wrigleyville neighborhood. Be patient, plan well, and allot a good amount of your day to absorb the stadium and the neighborhood. Despite the sometimes uncomfortable confines, Wrigley Field is truly one of the bucket-list places to go in all of baseball.

Ballpark Facts, Figures, & Tips

At one time during the Depression, select Cubs personnel lived in a spacious apartment at the ballpark. The "apartment" now holds the offices of the food service contractor…The original scoreboard installed by the legendary Bill Veeck in 1937 did not have a clock until 1941…Veeck was also responsible for planting the bucolic ivy on the outfield walls in 1937… The distinguishably unique foul poles have fencing in yellow paint displaying the distance of each line…The foul poles also feature the words "Hey Hey" in honor of the late announcer Jack Brickhouse…The "Bleacher Bums" were formed in the late 1960s by a group of rowdy fans who lived and died with the Cubs every home game. Their legend grew with the 1969 season and a 1977 play whose cast and writing team included Joe Mantegna…The ballpark has gone through a number of small and large renovations…Statues outside of the ballpark honor third baseman, humanitarian, and Hall of Famer Ron Santo and announcer Harry Caray.

 Best Tips for Seating

Wrigley Field is classically beautiful, but it is not modernly comfortable. Efforts have been made to convert the bias of the seats in the main grandstand lower level to have a bias toward home plate, but the Friendly Confines are confined to allow only so much leeway to do so. Box seats are expensive and premium pricing has been liberally used by the organization over the past few years because of demand.

However, demand is petering off of late and the Ricketts family is smart enough to know how to make the turnstiles work. By all indications, a pullback on premium pricing is afoot and family packages on the lower level are becoming a reality.

If you want to sit in the bleachers, plan well ahead of time if it is a weekend game you are attending. Especially if it is a weekend game between May 15 and Labor Day weekend. Chicagoans love their summer and the adjacent neighborhoods of Lakeview (aka Wrigleyville) have a high density of recent college graduates who plan their summers around Cubs home games. Thus, the price of a bleacher ticket most of the season is not affordable to bums anymore.

You will pay a commodity price for weekends and the price of a bleacher ticket during the week for a non-premium game will run fans almost $40.00 for a daytime game. Relief comes at night, though: a bleacher ticket can be grabbed for about $20.00 for a non-premium series.

Do not buy tickets in the 500 level if you have medical conditions that may bring on vertigo or if you plan on having a beer or two. The aisles are narrow and the stairways are steep and inconsistent. The higher you go at Wrigley Field, the less comfortable you are. Once you sit down, the view is incredible: the green of the grass, the brick-dust red infield, and the blue of Lake Michigan peeking over limestone apartment buildings. But you will have to get up again.

Once standing, you will have to traipse the stairs downward with great caution. If you are a male going to the restroom, you will be greeted with a line and forced to use a trough (it may be homage to the efficiency of Chicago's stockyard era… only without the efficiency). The ladies will get their own line at the restroom that will get epic reference at dinner party conversations among their friends about the worst line for the worst bathroom they ever endured. Both genders will get at least an inch of water on the floors. Avoid wearing flip flops or sandals.

Check out www.chicago.cubs.mlb.com and prepare yourself for the labyrinth that is the Chicago Cubs pricing schedule. Your heart says, "Hey, check out the availability of tickets for the Cardinals series!" with glee and excitement, then you find four tickets available in the 500 section and the price knocks you over. If you are shocked at the price, lower your expectations and aim lower in the standings. Premium pricing will not apply to a good amount of the series the Cubs play at Wrigley Field, and your odds of avoiding the upper levels of the grandstand will improve.

Driving Directions/Public Transportation

Wrigley Field is located at 1060 W. Addison, better known to Chicago locals as the corner of Clark and Addison. If you plan on driving to Wrigley Field, avoid driving to Wrigley Field. Parking has started going north of $50.00 for blocks around the area and the foot traffic rules traffic patterns the closer you get to the stadium. There are parking lots west of Southport Ave. (five blocks west of Wrigley Field) that will offer you a healthy walk, but you won't regret using them after you see the postgame congestion around the ballpark. System Parking at 3535 N. Ashland Ave. offers you one of the easiest routes away from the congestion at a price that won't break the bank.

If you plan on flagging down a cab from your hotel, make sure you plot out a drop-off point well away from the ballpark. A good drop-off point south of the stadium is Clark St. and Sheffield Ave. It's just far enough away from the ballpark that

you will get dropped off with no congestion. That is, as long as you get to the area no less than one hour before the game. Cabs from downtown Chicago to Wrigley Field will run a fan $30.00 to $35.00 (tip included).

Cabs after the ballgame are next to impossible to get immediately. Patience will be required and there are a lot of distractions for families and revelers alike to burn time after the game. Check out any number of memorabilia, merchandise, and swag shops around the ballpark and enjoy your time. You are going nowhere for a while. The good news is that cabs in Chicago are well-regulated and all pricing is virtually the same from cab to cab, company to company. Just make sure not to get sick in a Chicago cab (a $50.00 fine mandated by city ordinance).

The best option for fans going to a game at Wrigley Field is public transportation. The Chicago Transportation Authority (the CTA) has an elevated train on their Red Line that gets off at Addison from the north (Evanston) and south (downtown/South Side). Crafty locals will take the Brown Line, get off at Southport Ave., and walk a few blocks in an effort to avoid the crowds that concentrate around the ballpark for hours before and after the game. The CTA's bus system is first class and you can choose from a dozen reliable routes that pass Lakeview/Wrigleyville from the north, south, and west (if you are coming from the east, you are in Lake Michigan).

Parking
The best advice I can give to people looking for the best parking near Wrigley Field is to tell them to use a cab or the CTA. Failing those individuals taking my advice, I recommend they get into the Wrigley Field area early and do a once-around on the market. If you find a $40.00 spot, jump on it—that is the market floor for pricing these days. You may see some $60.00 lots closer to the stadium, but the medium price

point for parking around Wrigley Field these days is $45.00 to $50.00.

If you are blessed to find a parking spot near Wrigley Field, be prepared to do one of two things: leave the game early or stick around until the postgame congestion clears out. Listening to the postgame show is fun, but not so fun stuck in traffic.

Airports

Chicago is home to two excellent airports that service almost every major- and middle-market city on the planet. O'Hare Airport (ORD) is located on the far northwest side of the city and Midway Airport (MDW) is on the far southwest side of the city. Large international and domestic carriers tend to run in and out of O'Hare Airport. The discount airlines typically run in and out of Midway Airport. Chicago is a big target market for miles programs and availability of seats is tight. However, those who plan well in advance avoid problems.

Car Rentals

Chicago's main airports are serviced by all major car rental companies. Reservations can be made through the company website, major travel websites, or by phone. The companies that serve each airport are listed below:

O'Hare Airport (ORD)
Ace - (acerentacar.com)
Advantage - (800) 777-5500
Alamo - (800) 327-9633
Avis - (800) 331-1212
Budget - (800) 527-7000
Dollar - (800) 800-4000
Enterprise - (800) 566-9249
Hertz - (800) 654-3131
National - (800) 227-7368
Thrifty - (800) 527-7075

Midway Airport (MDW)
Advantage - (800) 777-5500
Alamo - (800) 327-9633
Avis - (800) 331-1212
Budget - (800) 527-7000
Dollar - (800) 800-4000
Enterprise - (800) 566-9249
Hertz - (800) 654-3131
National - (800) 227-7368
Thrifty - (800) 527-7075

 Hotels/Accommodations

Chicago has hundreds of hotels, and planning in advance has everything to do with whether or not you get the best experience for the best price. Plan too late and you are likely to find a good to great experience that will cost you a lot of money. Plan ahead and you may be paying hundreds of dollars less than the procrastinators.

You can find a traditional hotel or look for the growing number of B&B's (bed & breakfast) that are popping up all over Chicago's central city. Below is a list of hotels and B&B's ranging from economy to luxury where deals in Chicago can be found with research and a little advanced planning.

Chicago Getaway Hostel—616 W. Arlington Place, Chicago, IL, 60614, (866) 925-4159
City Suites Hotel—933 W. Belmont Ave., Chicago, IL, 60657, (866) 678-6350
The Drake Hotel—140 E. Walton Pl., Chicago, IL, 60611, (866) 539-5067
Hotel Indigo—1244 N. Dearborn Pkwy., Chicago, IL, 60610, (866) 538-1314
Hotel Lincoln—1816 N. Clark St., Chicago, IL, 60614, (866) 925-8676

SIDE TRIP: CHICAGO AND ILLINOIS CEMETERIES PLAY HOME TO MANY BASEBALL GREATS

It sounds a little ghoulish, but some baseball history can be appreciated with a simple walk through the graveyard. When in Chicago, take some time to pay respects to a few Hall of Famers:

William Hulbert (1832–1882), an original owner of the Chicago White Stockings (who became the Cubs), is buried a few blocks north of Wrigley Field at Graceland Cemetery. You cannot miss his grave: the centerpiece on his gravestone is a baseball. Hulbert wasn't enshrined in Baseball's Hall of Fame until 1995.

1939 Hall of Famer "Old Hoss" Radbourn (1853–1895) of recent Twitter fame (if you haven't seen it, check it out at @ oldhossradbourn—witty stuff) is buried in Evergreen Memorial Cemetery in Bloomington, Illinois. Old Hoss won 59 games in 1883 and gained quite the reputation as a cad on and off the field.

White Sox great Ray Schalk (1892–1970), who was widely credited with revolutionizing the catching position before the modern era, is buried in Evergreen Cemetery. Schalk entered the Hall of Fame in 1955.

The first commissioner of baseball, Kenesaw Mountain Landis (1866-1944), is buried in Oak Woods Cemetery (1035 E. 67th St., Chicago/South Side). Landis put a cap on gambling in baseball by creating Rule 21, sealing the fate of a lifetime ban for eight Chicago White Sox from the 1919 team and, 70 years later, Pete Rose.

Inn at Lincoln Park—601 W. Diversey Pkwy., Chicago, IL, 60614, (866) 767-0278

PUBLIC Chicago—1301 N. State Pkwy., Chicago, IL, 60610, (866) 538-6252

Sofitel Water Tower—20 E. Chestnut St., Chicago, IL, 60611, (866) 582-3258

The Westin Michigan Avenue—909 N. Michigan Ave., Chicago, IL, 60611, (866) 925-4218

The Whitehall Hotel—105 E. Delaware Pl., Chicago, IL, 60611, (866) 539-9234

Dining/Bars/Nightlife

Chicago is widely known as one of the best culinary cities in the world. You can find food from just about every culture and nationality, even different cultures within certain nationalities.

Or you can grab a steak or a set of pork chops at an excellent chop house (Chicagoans call a steak house a "chop house." The roots of the term "chop house" go back centuries and it stands locally as a reference to the salad days of the Union Stockyards (if slaughterhouses can have salad days). At one time, Chicago was "Hog Butcher to the World" (all credit to poet Carl Sandburg) and butchered the bulk of mass-produced hogs and cattle in the United States. Using the term "chop house" will lend you credibility with a concierge in Chicago.

However, your appetite will have many options in Chicago to consider. A few above-par bars have been included for your pregame prep or postgame celebration, too. Below is a list of restaurants that range from expensive to just plain cheap that will satisfy your taste buds:

The Art of Pizza—3033 N. Ashland Ave., Chicago, IL, 60657 (Pizza)
Azteca De Oro—3731 N. Clark St., Chicago, IL, 60613 (Mexican)
Bernie's Tap & Grill—3664 N. Clark St., Chicago, IL, 60613 (Bar/Grill)
Crosby's Kitchen—3455 N. Southport, Chicago, IL, 60657 (American)
El Nuevo—2914 N. Clark St., Chicago, IL, 60657 (Mexican)
Guthrie's Tavern—1300 W. Addison St., Chicago, IL, 60613 (Bar)
Half Shell—676 W. Diversey Pkwy., Chicago, IL, 60614 (Seafood/Cocktail)
Mia Francesca—3311 N. Clark St., Chicago, IL, 60657 (Italian)
New England Seafood Company—3341 N. Lincoln Ave., Chicago, IL, 60657 (Seafood)

Tango Sur—3763 N. Southport Ave., Chicago, IL, 60613 (Argentine/Steak)
Taverna 750—750 W. Cornelia St., Chicago, IL, 60657 (Italian/Cocktails)
Thai Classic Restaurant—3332 N. Clark St., Chicago, IL, 60657 (Thai)

Ballpark/Neighborhood Security

Yes, you are in a big city. No, you are not in a dangerous neighborhood. Lakeview and Wrigleyville are no different than any neighborhood you might encounter in your hometown. Take the same precautions you do at home for security and you should be fine at any time in this area of Chicago.

Police patrols are a constant presence around the ballpark. The Chicago Police Department is more concerned about traffic flow and crowd control than the game. This doesn't mean they are not watching the revelers. Drunks and people who try to take open containers out of a bar are just easy pickings. The CPD will arrest you and your $100 afternoon will have turned into a $10,000 afternoon. Be smart, keep your nose clean, and think twice before getting out of control.

A few blocks directly east of Wrigley Field is the center of the largest gay neighborhood in the Midwest (East Lakeview aka Boys Town). Boys Town is routinely known as one of the safest areas of the city. The community groups and neighborhood watch programs are very active and aware that safety is priority number one.

East Lakeview, once a grouping of deteriorating homes and businesses on Halsted Street, has been brought back to life with gentrification by the mostly gay community over the past 25 years. Every year the Pride Parade on the third weekend in June draws 2 million watchers. Be forewarned: traffic is not the best in this area if there is a Cubs series on Pride Weekend.

U.S. CELLULAR FIELD
Home of the Chicago White Sox

333 W. 35th St., Chicago, IL, 60616
(312) 674-1000 or (866) SOX-GAME (tickets)
http://chicago.whitesox.mlb.com and www.tourismchicago.org

Go to Chicago and ask someone the directions to U.S. Cellular Field and you might get a delay before you get your answer. Most people in Chicago still call the ballpark at 35th and Shields "Comiskey Park" or just "Comiskey." Younger fans have adapted to the world of corporate naming deals, but longtime White Sox fans (born before 1990) remember old Comiskey Park (1910–1990) with mixed emotions.

Old Comiskey Park was a classic baseball shrine built for the people of Chicago by the "Old Roman," owner Charles Comiskey, and was opened in 1910. Thereafter, the new ballpark became home to a White Sox ballclub that was a perennial American League challenger culminating in a World Series trophy in 1917. The ballpark even hosted the 1918 World Series between the crosstown-rival Chicago Cubs and Boston's mighty Red Sox because Comiskey Park had a larger seating capacity.

The White Sox then made it back to the World Series in 1919 and the effort—or purposeful lack of effort—would become a defining point in baseball history. Eight of the White Sox players were in cahoots with East Coast gamblers and aided in throwing the World Series to the Cincinnati Reds, five games to three games.

White Sox–great Joe Jackson was implicated in the conspiracy, but his numbers indicate that he was a better double-crosser than gambler's pawn. Jackson batted .375 in the 1919 World Series (21 points higher than his career average of .356) and committed no errors. Many historians have opined that Jackson took the money ($5,000.00) but never took a fall because his seven co-conspirators were doing a fine job handing the Reds the World Series.

In 1990, "New Comiskey" offered fans a new stadium to go along with their great history. The $150 million stadium was designed by HOK Sport to be functional, not emotional, for fans. White Sox fans that experienced old Comiskey Park remember the good times, but were not fond of the dripping rust from the ancient steel beams. The bathrooms were flooded more often than not. The players hated the ballpark. Fans hated the obstructed views. The new Comiskey Park would be as modern as old Comiskey was outdated.

If a poll were to be taken among White Sox fans, not only would a majority have approved a new ballpark but also volunteered to swing the first wrecking ball. Truth is, a lot of White Sox fans likely worked on the construction of the new ballpark and the razing of the old ballpark. This gives us a segue to Chicago baseball sociology.

I once asked my father why the Cubs have more day games than the White Sox. His response was simple, but to the point: "White Sox fans work for a living, Tim." Chicago White Sox fans have a friendly rivalry with Chicago Cubs fans, but the teams' fan bases have vastly different religious, ethnic, and economic roots. The lines are blurring with new generations and a changing America. However, my father's words still have a basis in sociology today.

In the first half of the 20th century, White Sox fans were more likely to be ethnic, Chicagoan by birth, Catholic, and Jewish. Cubs fans grew out of a cluster of neighborhoods on the North Side of Chicago that was northern European, white, and protestant. White Sox fans read the *Daily American* or *Sun-Times*. Cubs fans read the *Tribune*. White Sox fans were labor union or small-shop owners. Cubs fans were mainly white collar and downtown professionals. White Sox fans lived on the South Side, Cubs fans roamed and ruled the North Side. With time and social change, lines blurred.

Fast forward to today; never mind geography and the old stereotypes that shaped Chicago baseball sociology. Today, you can even find the occasional White Sox fan in a "Cubs family" and vice-versa. Truth be told, you find fewer and fewer fans of either team that hates the other team. That is especially the case with younger adults. The rigidity of the past may be going away. Blame it on interleague play, I guess.

There is a hard, fast rule obeyed by both sides of the Chicago baseball divide: no ketchup on a hot dog! Ketchup is offered at U.S. Cellular Field, but you will get grief for it if you are over the age of six. I once watched a Yankees fan get pilloried by the White Sox faithful for putting ketchup on their hot dog. Hot dogs, Polish sausage, and other Midwestern encased meats are treated like a religion at U.S. Cellular Field. Fans get offered two incredible brands of hot dogs at U.S. Cellular Field (Bobak's and Vienna).

If Wrigley Field offers a limited menu, U.S. Cellular Field's menu is anything but limited. Yes, hot dogs, pizza, and nachos are served. But the quality of encased meat (Bobak's & Vienna) is top notch. South Side fans will sit on their hands rather than reach for a mediocre pizza slice. Nachos? Fans can get their choice of Mexican nachos served in a black White Sox helmet or Irish nachos (waffle fries in lieu of tortilla chips) which is served in a green White Sox helmet.

Cuban sandwiches, Chinese bao, Burger Barn hamburgers that will fill you for two days, and burritos are offered on the U.S. Cellular Park menu. The best approach is to get to the game early and walk the U.S. Cellular concourse a few times. The options are plenty and the food is pretty good.

Before you go into the ballpark, check out the tent near Gate 5. The Bacardi in the Park facility offers premium drinks and specialty beer for fans coming into the ballpark. Their competition is about 100 yards away, though. The parking lots at Chicago's U.S. Cellular Field offer a top-five tailgate experience for Major League Baseball fans. If you are coming in by car regionally, tailgating is a great way to extend the quality of your White Sox game experience.

Crowds are not a big problem at U.S. Cellular Field. Even in the World Series year of 2005, sellouts were not the norm until late June at U.S. Cellular Field. Tickets should be available for weekday games at the ticket window. Deals can be found all over the White Sox website (www.chicago.whitesox.mlb.com) for the smart fan. Family deals and great group ticket prices are available for all 81 home games.

You will have a great time at U.S. Cellular Field. Set aside a few hours before the game for a tailgate with family and friends and enjoy an American League baseball game within just a few miles of Chicago's Loop.

Ballpark Facts, Figures, & Tips

The tradition of "The Star-Spangled Banner" being played at ballgames started at Comiskey Park in 1918…A marker representing where home plate was at old Comiskey Park rests in the parking lot north of Gate 5 at U.S. Cellular Field… Construction began in May of 1989 and the first game was played at the new building on April 18, 1991…The park was informally named Comiskey Park from 1991 to 2003 when U.S. Cellular (a telecommunications company) paid $68 million for the naming rights to the ballpark for the next 23 years…In their inaugural season at the new ballpark, the White Sox drew

2,934,154 fans…The Plumber's Union sponsors a shower on the center-field concourse. This is a nod to former owner Bill Veeck's installing a shower at the ballpark in the 1970s… Former organist Nancy Faust started the tradition of playing "Na Na Hey Hey Kiss Him Goodbye" in the 1970s when opposing teams changed pitchers…The 1959 Chicago White Sox (the Go-Go Sox) get homage throughout the game when the anthem "Go-go White Sox" is played in the shadow of a White Sox home run or base-clearing hit…The stadium is technically known as U.S. Cellular Field at Comiskey Park.

Best Tips for Seating

In the early 2000s, the Illinois Stadium Authority and the White Sox organization lopped off the top seven rows of the upper deck. Some would say this was 12 years overdue. The upper deck at U.S. Cellular Field is incredibly steep. Steepness aside, the top rows that were eliminated often went unused. Be very careful when you walk up the upper deck at U.S. Cellular Field. A person with a fear of heights would have a difficult time up there.

The bleachers at U.S. Cellular Field are underrated. You have full exposure to the sunshine during the day and a very good view of the field in most sections at night. The Private Bank Fan Deck sits in dead center field above the hitter's eye that has full concessions and four-top tables. Fans have a lot of options in this area and a wide concourse to get them anywhere on the first level.

That is another issue. You are limited to the level your ticket states and cannot roam around the entire stadium. Sitting in section 313 then, you only have access to section 300. There are reasons this is done, but ballpark aficionados do not have a friend in the designers and security staff of U.S. Cellular Field.

All seats in the ballpark have a bias toward the infield and you will be comfortable in your seat. The lower-deck rows are typically eight to 10 seats long. The aisles are abundant and fans do not have to constantly get up and down because they have 50 fans to a row.

The Miller Lite Bullpen in right field is a bar connected to a party deck that translates to a pretty good value and view for fans. Groups can rent out the Patio deck in right-center field for larger events. Lucky fans behind home plate sit, eat, and drink in luxury: the Magellan Scout seats are incredible. A very expensive ticket gets you a private full buffet and open bar below the grandstands plus table service at your seat. A lot of stadiums have gone to this level of service and Chicago definitely does it right.

Driving Directions/Transportation

From any highway that comes from the north, south, or west of Chicago, you will have to get to I-94 (known locally as the Dan Ryan Expressway). Once on I-94, you will want to get off at one of three exits: 47th Street, 35th Street (main), or 31st Street. The stadium can be seen just south of 35th Street on the west side of I-94.

Traffic management will flow you into the ballpark's many parking areas. As always, get to the ballpark earlier than later. Traffic on Opening Day and major series can get hairy and the overflow lot is two miles away on the grounds of McCormick Place.

As for public transportation, the Chicago Transit Authority (the CTA) Red Line lets off at 35th Street to the east of the ballpark. A CTA Green Line stop is on the Illinois Institute of Technology campus a few hundred yards east of the Red Line stop. The regional train system called Metra has a platform to the west of the ballpark. Always look to the trip planner pages for the CTA (www.transitchicago.com) and Metra (www.metrail.com) before heading out for the day to the ballgame.

Another source of public transportation for the region is the South Shore Railroad (NICTD) that services a line from South Bend, Indiana, to Chicago. The South Shore has a stop at McCormick Place and a cab can be grabbed from there to get to U.S. Cellular Field.

If you are going to U.S. Cellular Field from the downtown Chicago area and opt for a cab, be forewarned that competition for a cab after the game is tough—especially at night. Cabs know there is not a lot of demand from U.S. Cellular Field after a game and can get fares downtown. Best advice: take the Red Line and the CTA if you can't land a cab after the game. You'll save $20.00.

Parking

There are eight large parking lots to the north, west, and south of the stadium that provide ample parking for $20.00 ($10.00 on family day games). The traffic management in the area is excellent and you will get off of the stadium grounds quickly. So, be prepared and know which way to go on I-94 before you leave.

Airports

Chicago is home to two excellent airports that service almost every major- and middle-market city on the planet. O'Hare Airport (ORD) is located on the far northwest side of the city and Midway Airport (MDW) is on the far southwest side of the city. Large, international and domestic carriers tend to run in and out of O'Hare Airport. The discount airlines typically run in and out of Midway Airport. Chicago is a big target market for miles programs and availability of seats is tight. However, those who plan well in advance avoid problems.

Car Rentals

Chicago's main airports are serviced by all major car rental companies. Reservations can be made through the company website, major travel websites, or by phone. The companies that serve each airport are listed below:

O'Hare Airport (ORD)
Ace - (website only: www.acerentacar.com)

Advantage - (800) 777-5500
Alamo - (800) 327-9633
Avis - (800) 331-1212
Budget - (800) 527-7000
Dollar - (800) 800-4000
Enterprise - (800) 566-9249
Hertz - (800) 654-3131
National - (800) 227-7368
Thrifty - (800) 527-7075

Midway Airport (MDW)
Advantage - (800) 777-5500
Alamo - (800) 327-9633
Avis - (800) 331-1212
Budget - (800) 527-7000
Dollar - (800) 800-4000
Enterprise - (800) 566-9249
Hertz - (800) 654-3131
National - (800) 227-7368
Thrifty - (800) 527-7075

Hotels/Accommodations
Best Western Grant Park—1100 S. Michigan Ave., Chicago, IL, 60605, (866) 925-4159
Central Loop Hotel—111 W. Adams St., Chicago, IL, 60603, (866) 925-0548
Chicago South Loop Hotel—11 W. 26th St., Chicago, IL, 60616, (866) 573-4235
Congress Hotel—520 S. Michigan Ave., Chicago, IL, 60605, (866) 539-5067
Essex Inn—800 S. Michigan Ave., Chicago, IL, 60605, (866) 538-0251
Holiday Inn—506 W. Harrison St., Chicago, IL, 60607, (866) 538-1314
Hyatt Regency McCormick Place—2233 S. Martin Luther King Dr., Chicago, IL, 60616, (866) 767-0278

Ramada Hyde Park—4900 S. Lake Shore Dr., Chicago, IL, 60615, (866) 925-8676
Travelodge—65 E. Harrison St., Chicago, IL, 60605, (866) 538-6252
Wyndham—500 S. Dearborn St., Chicago, IL, 60605, (866) 538-9298

Dining/Bars/Nightlife

Chicago is a food city and when you're talking about the South Side you're talking about meat and potatoes, stick-to-your-ribs fare. A few really comfortable Bridgeport bars have been listed as well. Below is a list of restaurants on the South Side and South Loop of Chicago that will not disappoint:

Buddy Guy's Legends—700 S. Wabash Ave., Chicago, IL, 60605 (Cajun/BBQ)
Calumet Fisheries—3259 E. 95th St., Chicago, IL, 60617 (Seafood)

El Milagro—2400 W. 21st Pl., Chicago, IL, 60608 (Mexican)

Gio's Café & Deli—2724 S. Lowe Ave., Chicago, IL, 60616 (Italian/Deli)

Ignotz—2421 S. Oakley Ave., Chicago, IL, 60608 (Italian)

Schnitzel King—Bridgeport, 308 W. 33rd St., Chicago, IL, 60609 (American)

South Coast Sushi Bar—1700 S. Michigan Ave., Chicago, IL, 60616 (Japanese)

Lao Sze Chuan—2172 S. Archer Ave., Chicago, IL, 60616 (Chinese)

Maxwell St. Depot—411 W. 31st St., Chicago, IL, 60616 (Hot Dogs/Pork Chop Sandwiches)

MingHin Cuisine—2168 S. Archer Ave., Chicago, IL, 60616 (Dim Sum)

Ricobene's—252 W. 26th St., Chicago, IL, 60616 (Italian/Sandwiches)

Schaller's Pump—3714 S. Halsted St., Chicago, IL, 60609 (Bar/American)

Shinnick's Pub—3758 S. Union Ave., Chicago, IL, 60609 (Bar)

Vito & Nick's Pizzeria—8433 S. Pulaski Rd., Chicago, IL, 60652 (Pizza)

 Ballpark/Neighborhood Security

U.S. Cellular Field at Comiskey Park is located in a neighborhood of south Chicago called Bridgeport. Historically, Bridgeport has been a politically powerful neighborhood. The Daley family of multi-generational mayoral fame lived a few blocks directly west of the ballpark. As a matter of fact, the house still remains in the ownership of the Daley family. Three blocks west of the ballpark is a district police station widely reputed as one of Chicago's best.

Bridgeport is a mainly Irish, somewhat Italian, and tad bit Lithuanian neighborhood feeling the push of gentrification over the past decade. Young entrepreneurs, young professionals, and artists have found good real estate investment

opportunities in Bridgeport starting just about the time the White Sox won the World Series. While the median age of Bridgeport decreased, the ticket sales to the newer, younger neighbors increased. Bridgeport was suddenly dealing with the same struggle Lakeview and Wrigleyville had in the early 1980s when the Cubs' fortunes started turning.

Crime statistics show a lower concentration of crime across the board in Bridgeport in most communities along the lakefront, North or South Side. Two main reasons may be the high concentration of police and firefighters living in Bridgeport and the political clout (as the locals call it) of neighborhood pols.

You will be safe in and around U.S. Cellular Field at Comiskey Park. Take the same precautions you do in your hometown and be just as careful as you would be any day of the year anywhere.

KANE COUNTY COUGARS/
FIFTH THIRD BANK BALLPARK

Midwest League (A) Affiliate of the Chicago Cubs

· ·

34W002 Cherry Lane, Geneva, IL, 60134 (at Kirk Road)

The Kane County Cougars organization is floating on Cloud Nine these days. The organization became an affiliate of the nearby Chicago Cubs and you can feel the difference around town. Locals are excited about watching the Cubs developing prospects and relishing in the prospect of increased economic development that will follow.

Geneva is known for antique hunting and has vibrant bed and breakfasts and boutique hotels to accommodate visitors looking for deals. Cubs general manager Jed Hoyer and club president Theo Epstein are sending a good number of young prospects to Kane County and the fans are coming out to see these players—hopefully a couple years before they see them in Wrigley Field.

A weekend in Geneva is no longer just golf for the guys and shopping for the ladies. A great deal for families or groups is Comfort Inn's Cougars Package (Room for four and four game tickets for $115.00). Check the schedule at www.kccougars.com and snap up one of these packages for a weekend in Geneva.

Dining/Bars/Nightlife

The Little Owl Restaurant (101 West State St., Geneva) has a great menu of Italian selections. Stop for a beer at **Stockholm's** (306 W. State St, Geneva/Midwest American). If you are a husband or boyfriend who needs to check on the score while the ladies shop, hit the **The Old Towne Pub** (201 W. State St., Geneva/Sports bar).

Hotels/Accommodations

Comfort Inn—1555 E. Fabyan Pkwy., Geneva, IL, 60134, (630) 208-8811

The Herrington Inn—15 South River Lane, Geneva, IL, 60134, (630) 208-7433

PEORIA CHIEFS/DOZER FIELD

Midwest League (A) Affiliate of the St. Louis Cardinals

730 Southwest Jefferson Street, Peoria, IL, 61605

Dozer Field, formerly O'Brien Field, is a tropical paradise in the Midwest. Palm trees were installed along the left-field concourse beyond the grassy berm a few years back. Needless to say, the trees look like palm trees in a town where it snows regularly: challenged.

The ballpark opened in 2002 and was built to be functional for the fans, players, and the city of Peoria. There are 20 suites at the ballpark, which has served as a great entertainment tool for hometown corporate partner Caterpillar. Caterpillar pitched in with corporate support when the naming rights ended with O'Brien Auto Group in 2011 (thus the name Dozer Field). The ballpark food is functional: hot dogs, brats, pork chop sandwiches, etc. You may want to grab dinner before you get to the ballpark.

Dining/Bars/Nightlife

Kelleher's Pub and Eatery (619 S.W. Water St., Peoria/Irish) is a solid Irish bar with a decent, hearty menu that has over 20 taps. **Richard's on Main** (311 Main St, Peoria/Midwest American) gives a lot of options to the middle-of-the-road palate. **Atagucci's** (2607 N. University St., Peoria/Pizza) offers locals and visitors alike great pizza.

Peoria is a "beer and a shot" town, so check out Yelp.com, swing a dead cat, and take in some local flavor.

Hotels/Accommodations

Embassy Suites—100 Conference Center Dr., East Peoria, IL, 61611, (866) 573-4235

Staybridge Suites—300 W. Romeo B Garrett Ave., Peoria, IL, 61605, (866) 538-0251

THE THOME FAMILY OF PEORIA

Major League great and Peoria native Jim Thome hit 612 home runs in the bigs in a career that spanned from 1991 to 2012. But Jim had to live up to the greatness of his grandmother Carolyn and her on-field exploits before being considered a big shot in Peoria.

As a matter of fact, he also had to live up to the standards set by his father Art, Grandpa Chuck, and Uncle Chuck.

The Thome family was known for their talents in American Softball Association (ASA) fast-pitch softball competition in a period that spanned from 1923 to 1968. Peoria and central Illinois was a hotbed of fast-pitch softball in the golden age of the sport. Aunt Carolyn landed a much-appreciated file clerk job at Caterpillar in the Depression at the age of 15. The job was hers partly because she understood the filing system at the heavy-equipment manufacturer and mostly because the factory team needed a hit machine. Her career 587 hits for the Caterpillar Diesels and the Pekin Lettes made her an ASA and Illinois State Hall of Famer.

Grandpa Chuck began cranking out hits in 1923 and was pinch-hitting as late as 1959. Grandpa Thome was also coach for many years of the highly competitive Hiram Walkers team.

Young Chuck and Jim's father Art played major softball for decades in the central Illinois leagues, bashing out hundreds of hits, too. Art played for the very talented Caterpillar Diesels and Chuck played for a few teams at the higher-level International Softball Congress.

Fast-pitch softball is extremely difficult to play. The mound is closer and a hitter must have great reaction time. The four Thomes combined for over 5,000 hits in their respective careers. The fast-pitch leagues have all but died. However, their influence will go into baseball's Hall of Fame with Jim Thome. Plus, this family produced one heck of a guy in Jim Thome.

Jim Thome will enter the Hall of Fame thinking about Grandma Carolyn, a Hall of Famer in her own right.

THE FRONTIER LEAGUE

The Frontier League is a non-affiliated baseball league for college players. The teams are located in Illinois, Kentucky, Missouri, Ohio, and Pennsylvania. The Frontier League even has a traveling team (The Frontier Greys). Most players are "adopted" by local residents and live in spare rooms provided by their adopting family for the summer. Companies who support the teams often provide part-time jobs for players. Many Baseball America top 500 prospects play in the Frontier League. With some research, you can find a player or two of interest and check them out with a short side trip as part of your planned baseball road trip. Below is a list of Frontier League teams located in the state of Illinois:

Southern Illinois Miners/Rent One Park
. . . .

1000 Miners Dr., Marion, IL, 62959
(618) 998-8499 / www.southernillinoisminers.com

This non-traditional ballpark has a design all its own. The 3,400-seat structure looks like a large block building up until you enter it and see it is a ballpark. Rent One Park is less than two hours south of St. Louis.

Gateway Grizzlies/GCS Ballpark
. . . .

2301 Grizzlie Bear Blvd., Sauget, IL, 62206
(618) 337-3000 / www.gatewaygrizzlies.com

GCS Ballpark boasts a capacity for almost 6,000 fans and has drawn over 200,000 a few years since opening in 2002. GCS Ballpark gained fame on the Travel Channel show *Man vs. Food* for its most unique food item: a bacon cheeseburger served on Krispy Kreme donuts.

Joliet Slammers/Silver Cross Field
. . . .

1 Mayor Art Schultz Dr., Joliet, IL, 60432
(815) 722-2287 / www.jolietslammers.com

This accommodating 6,016-seat stadium was built in 2002. The steel-and-red-brick traditional style ballpark is comfortable for fans and players alike. Two major rail lines for Chicagoland's Regional Transit Authority (METRA) have stops within a short walk of Silver Cross Field.

Normal CornBelters/The Corn Crib

1000 W. Raab Rd., Normal, IL, 61761
(309) 454-BALL / www.normalbaseball.com

Opened in 2010, The Corn Crib is a multi-purpose stadium with a capacity of 7,000. The Corn Crib is known for its ability to draw crowds with entertainment beyond the baseball field.

Rockford Aviators/Road Ranger Stadium

4503 Interstate Blvd., Loves Park, IL, 61111
(815) 885-2255 / www.rockfordaviators.com

This 3,300-seat stadium has a beautifully designed façade that welcomes fans to a comfortable ballpark experience. Rockford is home to a few major trucking companies who are supportive of the Aviators. Road Ranger Stadium boasts one of the bigger scoreboards in the Frontier League.

Schaumburg Boomers/Boomers Stadium

1999 S. Springinsguth Rd., Schaumburg, IL, 60193
(847) 461-3695 / www.boomersbaseball.com

Boomer Stadium is within 25 miles of Chicago off of the I-94 expressway and surrounded by the growing suburb of Schaumburg. The Boomers host some of the most fun and unique giveaway nights. There is a regular schedule of Thirsty Thursdays and fireworks nights to draw groups and families to this 7,365-seat ballpark.

Windy City ThunderBolts/Standard Bank Stadium

14011 S. Kenton, Crestwood, IL, 60445
(708) 489-2255 / www.wcthunderbolts.com

The 3,200-seat Standard Bank Stadium boasts a beer garden and a kids zone. The uniquely designed ballpark draws a crowd mainly from Crestwood, a neighborhood within Chicago's far South Side. Standard Bank Stadium also hosts concerts and varying types of festivals.

THE MIDWEST COLLEGIATE LEAGUE

The Midwest Collegiate League is a non-affiliated baseball league for college players. The teams are located in Illinois and Indiana. Most players are "adopted" by local residents and live in spare rooms provided by their adopting family for the summer. Companies who support the teams often provide part-time jobs for players. Many Baseball America top 750 prospects play in the league. With some research, you can find a player or two of interest and check them out with a short side trip as part of your planned baseball road trip. Below is a list of Midwest Collegiate League teams located in the state of Illinois:

DuPage County Hounds/
Village of Lisle-Benedictine Univ. Field

5700 College Rd., Lisle, IL, 60523
(815) 704-3839 / www.dupagehounds.com

This 1,100-seat stadium fills a dual role as the regular season home of the Benedictine University baseball team and the Hounds.

Rockford Foresters/Marinelli Field

101 15th Ave., Rockford, IL, 61104
(815) 312-2115 / www.rockfordforesters.com

Marinelli Field, a 2,357-seat ballpark, hosts the Foresters in a two-team town. The Rockford Aviators play at crosstown Road Ranger Stadium. Time will tell if both teams can survive or will co-exist at Road Ranger Stadium for economic development reasons.

Chicago Zephyrs/Waubonsee Community College

3 South 517 Winfield Rd., Warrenville, IL, 60555
(630) 327-9295 / www.zephyrs-baseball.com

The Chicago Zephyrs use the name of the old NBA club that once played in Chicago in the early 1960s. The 1,000-seat stadium draws small- to medium-sized crowds to the community college stadium. Warrenville is within a few miles and highway ramps from Fifth Third Bank Ballpark and the Kane County Cougars.

Southland Vikings/Flossmoor High School Field

999 Kedzie Ave., Flossmoor, IL, 60422
(708) 798-9572 / www.southlandvikings.com

The Southland Vikings effectively play on a larger than usual high school ballpark. Five hundred fans can fit into the bleachers at this suburban Chicago outpost in the Midwest Collegiate League.

Lexington Snipes/High Desert Field

600 N. Oak St., Lexington, IL, 61753
www.lexingtonsnipes.com

High Desert Field plays home to one of the best named ballclubs in the Midwest Collegiate League. The Snipes welcome as many as 1,100 fans to their not-so-permanent ballpark. Lexington is off Interstate 55 and Route 66 traverses through this central Illinois town.

CHAPTER 2

INDIANA

· ·

Baseball from Lake Michigan to the Ohio River

VICTORY FIELD
HOME OF THE INDIANAPOLIS INDIANS

AAA Affiliate of the Pittsburgh Pirates/
International League

. . . .

501 W. Maryland St, Indianapolis, IN, 46225
(317) 269-3545 / www.indyindians.com

The people of the city of Indianapolis have a jewel in Victory Field in their downtown stadium district. In the shadow of the Colts' Lucas Oil Stadium and a stone's throw from the Pacers' Bankers Life Fieldhouse is Victory Field. Indianapolis is the third largest major city in the United States without a major league baseball team (first is San Antonio, second is San Jose). Victory Field is anything but minor league in its design and comfort.

Designed by Huber, Hunt, and Nichols, Victory Field has set standards for all other new minor league ballparks for almost two decades. Within just a few years of being open, *Baseball America* and *Sports Illustrated* named Victory Field the "Best Minor League Baseball Stadium in America." The mold was certainly broken when Victory Field opened its gates in July of 1996.

Victory Field is another reason to take a long weekend in Indianapolis. The downtown area alone offers large city-level hotels, shopping, and restaurants without the crowds or congestion of a large city. Granted, the metropolitan Indianapolis area has over a million people. However, the generous amount of land and the lack of a major waterway gave the city planners the ability to spread things out a bit.

Victory Field is at the corner of Maryland and West Streets in the southwest quadrant of the downtown area. The stadium was built for $20 million and that comes off as a bargain these days compared to newer stadiums being built. Victory Field replaced Bush Stadium, which sat on the White River, lost between the downtown center and the famed Indianapolis Motor Speedway. Bush Stadium (originally

Perry Stadium) was a classic pre-Depression-era stadium that hosted many minor league championship teams and played host to a young Hank Aaron, who played for the Indianapolis Clowns of the Negro Leagues.

Bush Stadium had become rough around the edges during the 1980s. The infrastructure of the ballpark was crumbling and repairs were becoming a regular event. An effort to increase revenue streams to finance the needed repairs included renting Bush Stadium out as a movie set. The ballpark served as a stand-in for Comiskey Park in John Sayles' movie *Eight Men Out*, starring John Cusack and John Mahoney.

But in the early 1990s the old girl finally showed signs that there would be no recovery and the Indianapolis–Marion County Council voted a financing package to build Victory Field. The crowds at Victory Field have gotten as high as 16,100, but the official capacity of the ballpark is 15,500. The expansive outfield berm reaches from one foul pole

to the other and offers fans a patch of grass for $5.00. The ballpark's grandstand is a unique multi-deck design where fans can watch the game from the concourse with no interruption as they gather food and drink from concessionaires.

Indianapolis businesses snap up one of the 28 luxury suites whenever they become available. There are five party decks on level with the suites for rent and the corporate picnic areas in left and right field are massive. To top it off, the seats in the grandstand are configured to lend themselves to the best angle of the game possible. So, when they say there isn't a bad seat in the house, they were talking about Victory Field.

SIDE TRIP: FINDING MORDECAI "THREE FINGER" BROWN

Mordecai "Three Finger" Brown not only has one of baseball's greatest nicknames ever, but he was also a native-born Hoosier. Cubs fans and baseball lovers make a regular homage to Brown's gravesite in Terre Haute, Indiana.

Three Finger's legend rests on the fact that he served as an anchor to the Cubs rotation in their pennant runs in the early 20th century. In 1908, Brown pitched a solid 11 innings and won two games to bring home the World Series trophy to Wrigley Field.

Mordecai Brown was elected to the Hall of Fame in 1949. Brown is buried in Roselawn Memorial Park in Terre Haute (7500 N. Clinton St.). Your GPS won't be too taxed: just take I-70 west from Indianapolis for an hour and fifteen minutes and Terre Haute is on the left.

Victory Field is a functional facility year-round and a part of the natural corporate campus that is White River State Park. The Eiteljorg Museum of Native American History, the NCAA Hall of Champions, the Indianapolis Zoo, and an IMAX theatre are all tucked within a triangle bordered by a river, a canal, and the campus of Indiana University–Purdue University at Indianapolis.

Along with the nickname "Crossroads of America," Indianapolis holds the title of "Amateur Sports Capital of the World." The stadiums and facilities from the downtown area onto the campus of the university itself look like the city is prepared to host the Olympics at a moment's notice. The Indiana University Natatorium, the Carroll Track & Soccer Stadium, and the professional stadiums all line up as you look northwest from above the city.

The skyline that goes from nearly foul pole to foul pole beyond the outfield fence is striking. The massive Marriott complex built across the street from the left-field fence for Super Bowl XLVI is an incredible place for travelers to make camp as they enjoy the Circle City. Many conventions are held through the year at the Indianapolis Convention Center, whose campus sits across the street from the right-field fence.

Victory Field will wow your taste buds with a unique menu and an excellent beer selection. Arni's Pizza is served (a central Indiana classic) and beers from Sun King Brewery can be found at Captain Morgan's Cove. You can build your own burger at the aptly named Build-a-Burger stand and your sweet tooth will dance for joy at

Rowdie's Ice Cream Shoppe (Rowdie is the Indians mascot). You can also enjoy the treasure that is an Indiana pork tenderloin sandwich at the Backstop Grille. Don't forget the pickles and mustard.

Checking out Victory Field is a must for any ballpark fan. The month of May has always been a light home schedule for the Indianapolis Indians because of the festivities surrounding the Indianapolis 500, but that just makes for more dates to attend games throughout the rest of the summer.

Television announcer and observer Bob Costas called Victory Field "a miniature Camden Yards or Coors Field" for its modern amenities with old-fashioned charm. He was right. Visit Indianapolis and Victory Field and you will be enjoying a cheaper than usual ballpark experience with all of the professionalism of a major league ballpark. You will thoroughly enjoy this wonderful marriage between a city and its ballpark.

Dining/Bars/Nightlife

Indy is a better food town than advertised. I would walk across the Sahara desert for a corned beef on rye from **Shapiro's Deli** (808 S. Meridian St., Indianapolis). Shapiro's is without a doubt the best deli in Indiana, maybe the Midwest.

For incredible Italian from a truly family-run restaurant, head over to **Iaria's** (317 S. College Ave.). Just south of that neighborhood is Fountain Square, a hip up-and-coming area of the city that offers excellent Greek food at a great price at **Santorini** (1417 Prospect St.).

For one of the best steaks in America, hit **St. Elmo's Steakhouse** (127 S. Illinois St.). The shrimp cocktail coated in horseradish sauce with a sidecar of beer back is among the items listed on this writer's last meal requests. If your budget is a little tighter and an Indiana pork tenderloin sandwich is calling your name, head to **Edward's Drive-In** (2126 S. Sherman Dr.) and get your pig on.

For high-density nightlife for the 21-to-34 set, a taxi or designated driver and a ride up to the Broad Ripple neighborhood is required. For David Letterman fans, you can do a drive-by viewing of his childhood home on Indianaola Ave. in Broad Ripple.

Hotels/Accommodations

J.W. Marriott—10 S. West St., Indianapolis, IN, 46204, (866) 573-4235

Fairfield Inn—501 W. Washington St., Indianapolis, IN, 46204, (866) 678-6350

Courtyard by Marriott—601 W. Washington St., Indianapolis, IN, 46204, (866) 767-0278

Directions/Transportation/Parking

Victory Field is accessible from both I-65 and I-70. The best route from the north, south, and east is I-65 to I-70 west to the West St. exit. From the west, it is a straight shot on I-70 to West St. Once on West St., head north and the signs will lead you to Victory Field.

Indianapolis is surrounded by a loop called I-465 and it is extremely easy to get anywhere quickly. That is, anywhere except the I-69 corridor. Growth is clogging this area up to a standstill during non-rush hours. A regional transit plan has been stalled for decades to solve the problem. Indianapolis is not a public transportation city.

SIDE TRIP: THE LIMESTONE LEAGUE: INDIANA'S SPRING TRAINING HISTORY

The Hoosier state was home to spring training in the early 1940s. In an effort to aid the war effort, cities and towns throughout the Hoosier state volunteered their towns to major league ballclubs. The league became known as the Limestone League. After the war, baseball decided to move toward training in Texas and Florida until the 1960s. The model moved toward the Arizona/Florida model we know today. Here is a list of teams and the towns in Indiana in which they trained in during the war:

- Chicago Cubs (French Lick)
- Chicago White Sox (French Lick and Terre Haute)
- Cincinnati Reds (Bloomington)
- Cleveland Indians (Lafayette)
- Detroit Tigers (Evansville)
- Pittsburgh Pirates (Muncie)

Source: The Limestone League: Spring Training in Indiana During WWII/Indiana Historical Society/Steve Krah/1997

Parking will not be an issue. Very cheap parking can be found all around the downtown area because the White River State Park, convention center, and sports stadiums were planned for events.

Airport: Indianapolis International Airport (IND)
Major Airlines: Yes (All major U.S. airlines and Air Canada)
Car Rentals: Yes (Within airport)

FORT WAYNE TINCAPS/ PARKVIEW FIELD

Midwest League (A) Affiliate of the
San Diego Padres
· ·
1301 Ewing St., Fort Wayne, IN, 46802

More than a few observers have conveyed to me that they attended a game at Parkview Field in Fort Wayne, Indiana, and were astonished the structure was built in 2009. The ballpark was designed to amaze fans with its detail. "Innovative" was the word used most by others to describe their experience at Parkview Field.

The brick architecture gives off a feeling that Parkview Field has been around 100 years. The comfortable seats and wide concourses say this is a new ballpark. The ballpark shows off Fort Wayne's skyline for sure. A bandshell in centerfield serves as somewhat of a conduit to the business district. Many professionals find time to take in lunch during day games that usually start around lunch time. Whether they go back to the office or not after an hour is a case-by-case situation. The decision is usually determined by the run differential and the weather.

One thing you will notice is how they tucked this ballpark into its surroundings. Despite the limited acreage, Parkview Field is efficient with its space and comfortable for fans. As for food, you have more options than your typical ballpark. Concession stands will offer you the traditional fare. However, a couple of dozen food carts dot the concourse and give fans choices of everything from Philly cheesesteaks to Mexican. Get used to apple offerings: Fort Wayne is the claimed resting place of Johnny Appleseed, the original Tincap. The Apple Cart on the home plate concourse offers apple juice, apple cobbler, and apple turnovers.

An abundance of history is featured on the concourse of Parkview Field. Plaques along the concourse outline Fort Wayne baseball history and the city's relevant baseball figures. A stroll along the concourse is informative and will open your eyes to one great ballpark. A visit to Fort Wayne's Parkview Field is a must-do for fans wanting to see a stadium at the cusp of innovation in baseball.

Dining/Bars/Nightlife

Fort Wayne has some pretty solid cuisine for a city its size. **Don Chava's** (234 N. Wells St., Fort Wayne) is a Mexican restaurant within a mile of the ballpark and a local favorite. **Don Hall's Old Gas Hall** (305 E. Superior St., Fort Wayne) serves solid traditional American fare and is open pre- and postgame.

Fort Wayne is somewhat of a sister city to Toledo, so coney dogs are naturally loved by the locals. **Coney Island Weiner Stand** (131 W. Main St., Fort Wayne) makes a solid coney dog. Eating just one takes enormous discipline. They are extremely good dogs. For nightlife, check out the classic dive bar called **The Brass Rail** (1121 Broadway, Fort Wayne). The Brass Rail has great local flavor within a blocks of the ballpark and beers won't break the bank.

Hotels/Accommodations

Courtyard by Marriott—1150 S. Harrison St., Fort Wayne, IN, 46802, (866) 573-4235
Stay Inn Suites—4919 Lima Rd., Fort Wayne, IN, 46808, (866) 767-0278
Best Western Luxury—5501 Coventry Ln., Fort Wayne, IN, 46804, (866) 925-8709

SOUTH BEND SILVER HAWKS/ COVELESKI STADIUM

Midwest League (A) Affiliate of the
Arizona Diamondbacks

501 W. South St., South Bend, IN, 46601

The South Bend Silver Hawks are going through somewhat of
a renaissance over the past five years. In the mid-2000s, the
franchise was considered to be dying on the vine. Then, a temporary
ownership group including the former mayor of South Bend worked
to rehabilitate the organization and strengthen the bones of Coveleski
Stadium. Once that job was complete, the Silver Hawks were sold to
Andrew T. Berlin, who looks to further improve the organization.

Coveleski Stadium was left in disrepair, to say the least. "The Cove"
improved the seating, entrances, and the suites with the ownership
change in 2012 and the stadium became more welcoming. Inflatable
bouncy games are set up in the outfield area and the Silver Hawks
store is set up for all of your swag needs in right field.

One of the reasons for decline in attendance between the mid-1990s
and mid-2000s had a lot to do with the switch in affiliations from the
nearby Chicago White Sox to the far-off Arizona Diamondbacks. South

Bend baseball fans root for the White Sox, Cubs, and somewhat for the Tigers. The Diamondbacks have had a difficult time gaining the loyalty of South Bend fans, even though the club had Brandon Webb and Justin Upton pass through the university town on the first stop of their careers.

South Bend is home to the University of Notre Dame. The Fighting Irish baseball team does not play at the ballpark but the student body takes the time to hit Silver Hawks games. Deals exist through the week at the Cove like Dollar Mondays and Thirsty Thursdays. Labor unions and corporations set aside nights to entertain their membership and employees on the weekend.

The food choices at the Cove are pretty much down the middle of the fairway: hot dogs, brats, chili dogs, etc. However, as is custom in Indiana, the menu goes up a couple notches with the pork tenderloin sandwich. Individual carts offer the more specialty food items. A great local microbrew named The Four Horsemen stands out above the corporate beer offerings on the menu. A great list of beer choices are offered at The Pine Tar Pub, too.

You are not getting cheated at Coveleski Field when it comes to the complete baseball experience. The atmosphere is great and you will feel welcomed by the great staff. The recent improvements structurally and within the marketing department will only make for a better ballpark experience in the future.

 Dining/Bars/Nightlife

The palate of South Bend has gone from the meat and potatoes of an industrial town to international. **Cambodian Thai** (229 S. Michigan St., South Bend) tickles the tongue with top-notch pan-Asian cuisine. You will feel the warmth of the home fires with a visit to the **Fiddler's Hearth** (127 N. Main St., South Bend). The Fiddler's Hearth is a taste of Ireland in the shadow of the home of the Fighting Irish.

If you want pizza, try **Barnaby's** (713 E. Jefferson Blvd., South Bend). The thin crust is on par with the classic thin crusts you find on the South Side of Chicago. For a nightcap, you can't avoid hitting **Corby's Irish Pub** (441 E. Lasalle Ave., South Bend). Just make sure it's early and the students haven't invaded the premises. Sports movie buffs may remember Corby's from the movie *Rudy*.

 Hotels/Accommodations

Holiday Inn Express—120 N. Dixie Way, South Bend, IN, (866) 925-8676

Quality Inn & Suites—4124 Lincoln Way W., South Bend, IN,
(866) 538-0251
Hilton Garden Inn—53995 St. Rte. 933, South Bend, IN,
(574) 232-7700

THE FRONTIER LEAGUE

The Frontier League is a non-affiliated baseball league for college players. The teams are located in Illinois, Kentucky, Missouri, Ohio, and Pennsylvania. The Frontier League even has a traveling team (The Frontier Greys). Most players are "adopted" by local residents and live in spare rooms provided by their adopting family for the summer. Companies who support the teams often provide part-time jobs for players. Many Baseball America top 500 prospects play in the Frontier League. With some research, you can find a player or two of interest and check them out with a short side trip as part of your planned baseball road trip. Below is a list of Frontier League teams located in the state of Indiana:

Evansville Otters/Bosse Field

1701 N. Main St., Evansville, IN, 47711
(812) 435-8686 / www.evansvilleotters.com

Bosse Field is a classic ballpark in this great Ohio River town. Built in 1915, Bosse Field is the third oldest continuously used ballpark in America. Evansville is also home to one of America's best barbeques: Wolf's BBQ. The journey through beautiful southern Indiana to Bosse Field is a throwback you will thoroughly enjoy.

THE AMERICAN ASSOCIATION OF INDEPENDENT PROFESSIONAL BASEBALL

The American Association of Independent Professional Baseball (AAIPB) was founded in 2005 after the Central League collapsed and greater definition came to the independent baseball landscape in North America. The geography of the AAIPB stretches down a central swath of North America from Winnipeg, Saskatchewan to Amarillo, Texas. Below are teams playing in the American Association of Independent Professional Baseball in Indiana:

Gary Southshore RailCats/U.S. Steel Yard

1 Stadium Dr., Gary, IN, 46402
(219) 882-2255 / www.railcatsbaseball.com

The people of the city of Gary and the northwest region of Indiana have a gem of a ballpark in U.S. Steel Yard. The two-tiered stadium holds 6,140 fans and hosts everything from Little League games up to the RailCats and major concert events. Opened in 2002, the U.S. Steel Yard has become a regular setting for NCAA baseball tournament events.

THE MIDWEST COLLEGIATE LEAGUE

The Midwest Collegiate League is a non-affiliated baseball league for college players. The teams are located in Illinois and Indiana. Most players are "adopted" by local residents and live in spare rooms provided by their adopting family for the summer. Companies who support the teams often provide part-time jobs for players. Many Baseball America top 750 prospects play in the league. With some research, you can find a player or two of interest and check them out with a short side trip as part of your planned baseball road trip. Below is a list of Midwest Collegiate League teams located in the state of Indiana:

Northwest Indiana Oilmen/Oil City Stadium

· ·

1700 119th St., Whiting, IN, 46394
(219) 659-1000 / www.nwioilmen.com

Oil City Stadium is an 800-seat ballpark that makes good use of a plot of Whiting, Indiana's, refinery district. The beautiful stadium green scoreboard and brick accents make this one of the best ballparks in the Midwest Collegiate League. The Oilmen also host a number of special nights that draw fans from all over the northwest Indiana region.

CHAPTER 3

IOWA

· · · · · · · · · · · · · · · · · · · ·

Cornfields, I-Cubs, and Fields of Dreams

PRINCIPAL PARK
HOME OF THE IOWA CUBS
AAA Affiliate of the Chicago Cubs
• •

1 Line Dr., Des Moines, IA, 50309
(515) 243-6111 / www.iowacubs.com

Where the Des Moines and Raccoon Rivers meet, Principal Park rises from the Iowa soil. Iowa's capitol is shown off like a prize pig at the Iowa State Fair beyond the outfield wall. The capacity of 11,500 seats and 45 suites are tested on an almost nightly basis. At an average attendance yearly of 486,000 fans since Principal Park was built in 1992, people do come. As James Earl Jones once famously said in a baseball movie about Iowa, they most certainly do come.

The Chicago Cubs have worked with the Iowa Cubs to create a top-flight minor league organization in Des Moines. Never mind the corporate amenities and fabulous grandstand, consider the goodies for families: four picnic areas, a kids play zone, a quaint fountain in right field, and a major league quality restaurant in right field.

Among Midwestern stadiums, few can match the variety of food offered by Principal Park. Of course, the Iowa pork tenderloin sandwich is offered in two sizes: the regular or massive $12.00 sewer lid of a sandwich. Iowans get a taste of a Chicago favorite with the offering of an Italian beef sandwich (add the peppers). If your yen is pork or beef of a different style, try Stu's BBQ for brisket or pulled pork. Want to really shock your friends and make them green with food envy: Principal Park offers bacon Sloppy Joes. Of course, you have the standard ballpark fare if adventure is not your game.

Most of your beer choices will be the major corporate brewers. Imports and microbrews are offered, too. What you will find a bit unusual is the walk-in refrigerator sponsored by Coors Light on the concourse. The Beer Box gives fans a choice of many types of canned beers in many sizes for the same prices of the drafts offered at the concession stands.

The bulk of the seating and luxury suites are in the main grandstand bowl. There is a set of bleachers in right field and a set of suites above the left-field wall. Every stadium has hits and misses, but not putting Chicago brick facades on the left-field suites that look like the buildings on Chicago's Waveland Avenue is a miss—maybe next time. Seats in the grandstand are very comfortable and bias toward the infield as they should.

One thing that will remind you of Chicago's Wrigleyville is the neighborhood that surrounds the ballpark. While there is not the bar upon bar, restaurant upon restaurant that you find around the parent club's stadium, you do have more choices than average for a good pre- or postgame bite or beer. Des Moines is a business center and a state capital, so your choices and views are better than most minor league cities.

The Budweiser Party Patio has one of the best views of the ballpark. The exclusivity of a suite is nice, but paying a fraction of that amount per ticket and being outside sounds much nicer on a hot Iowa night. The right-field bleachers look tempting, but once again, another miss: they should reconfigure these seats upon their next redesign to look more like Wrigley's bleachers than a portable grandstand at a high school football field.

The façade of the park's exterior could also use a dose of "Wrigleyfication." After all, the I-Cubs (as they are known by the Cubs faithful) draw fans from a wider reach than your average AAA team. The Cubs fan base in North America is massive and their local appeal in Iowa is unrivaled.

Despite the few design deficiencies, this is a great ballpark. Sitting, standing, or walking, you will be comfortable at Principal Park.

Take the time and hit the road to Des Moines. A good chunk of America is within a reasonable drive to Iowa's capital. There are also dozens of flights into and out of Des Moines International Airport daily. Typically, you wouldn't think of Des Moines as a vacation spot. However, it is a good starting point for a baseball road trip around a state full of great ballparks and full of baseball history.

 Dining/Bars/Nightlife

Des Moines is a food town. Iowa is a food state. You will not be disappointed by the offerings presented. This is the bread basket of America, after all. **Tumea & Sons** (1501 SE 1st St., Des Moines) offers tasty rustic Italian food. For solid Tex-Mex, hit the hip **El Bait Shop** (200 SW 2nd St., Des Moines) for fajitas.

When in Iowa, do as the Iowans do: find a pork tenderloin sandwich. The most recommended place for such a sammie is **The High Life** (200 SW 2nd St., Des Moines). The High Life is a hipster dive that draws all types. For a nightcap of German beer, hit **Hessen Haus** (101 4th St., Des Moines).

Hotels/Accommodations
Renaissance Savery—401 Locust St., Des Moines, IA, (866) 573-4235
Embassy Suites—101 E. Locust St., Des Moines, IA, (866) 678-6350
Hyatt Place—418 6th Ave., Des Moines, IA, (866) 767-0278

Airport: (DSM) **Major Airlines:** Y **Car Rentals:** Y

SIX MINOR LEAGUE TOWNS IN SIX DAYS

The state of Iowa may not have a Major League Baseball team, but the state offers a seven-day minor league road trip unto itself.

First, start in Des Moines. You can fly in or drive, but the state capitol of Iowa makes a great starting point for a five-city baseball road trip that includes all five Iowa major minor league cities. While in Des Moines, enjoy an Iowa Cubs game at Principal Park. Stay the evening in Des Moines and rest up: a long trip in a short time starts on Day 2.

The key to planning is plotting out when teams are transitioning road trips and homestands. Investigate the websites of each team. Two to three teams will be home at the same time. Starting on a Tuesday works because Thursday or Friday will be when teams transition homestands and road trips. If you plan on straddling homestands among the lot of teams, things will likely work to your favor in completing the five-city tour. There are multiple opportunities every night to see minor league baseball in Iowa.

Below is a sample of travel legs between cities with driving directions for major highways. In total, you will drive a minimum of 480 miles.

Day 1: Arrive in Des Moines. Drive to the Bob Feller Museum in the afternoon and Principal Park that evening for an Iowa Cubs game.

Day 2: Des Moines to Cedar Rapids—115 miles (I-80E to 380N) to see the Cedar Rapids Kernels at the new Veterans Memorial Stadium.

Day 3: Cedar Rapids to Clinton—84 miles (S.R. 30 East) to see the Clinton Lumber Kings at Ashford University Field.

Day 4: Clinton to Davenport—37 miles (S.R. 67S to I-80W) to see the Quad Cities River Bandits at Modern Woodmen Park.

Day 5: Davenport to Burlington—79 miles (74E thru IL to S.R. 34W) to see the Burlington Bees at Community Field.

Day 6: Burlington to Des Moines—161 miles (S.R. 218N to I-80W).

CEDAR RAPIDS KERNELS/ NEW VETERANS MEMORIAL STADIUM

Midwest League (A) Affiliate of the Minnesota Twins

· ·

950 Rockford Road SW, Cedar Rapids, IA, 52404 / (800) 860-3609

Perfect Game Field at Veterans Memorial Stadium is commonly known in Cedar Rapids as "new" Veterans Memorial Stadium. The new incarnation of the ballpark was opened in 2002. Cedar Rapids is a town of tough people. They are our farmers; they build weapons systems and assemble kitchen appliances. The people of Cedar Rapids work hard and play hard. The ballpark is their summertime outlet for a good time.

Veterans Memorial Stadium was a barebones stadium before the rebuild in 2001–02. The new parking lot is where the old stadium stood. The ballpark has a lot of charm, but the man-made noise never ends. Be forewarned that the Cedar Rapids Kernels have adopted the philosophy that you have a short attention span and that your ears and eyes constantly need to be fed. While I prefer announcements to be limited to the batter's name and the occasional organ music as I update my scorecard, Cedar Rapids knows they are in the entertainment business and that includes families with children who need their attention stoked.

The new ballpark gets high marks for the seating (there isn't a bad one among the 5,400 seats). The bowl grandstand holds the vast majority of seats, but there is a small cluster of bleachers behind the left-field wall. As with most Midwest League stadiums, the walls are half-inch plywood four-by-eight sheets with advertisements from local businesses. The field was updated with the rebuild, as well.

After you park, you will be routed to the main gate, which is positioned in the left-field corner. Concession stands serve standard ballpark fare and are abundant along the concourse of the grandstand. You will also run into occasional reminders throughout the ballpark of ballplayers who made the majors and went on to great careers that made stops in Cedar Rapids. The experience will be comfortable, but loud. Cedar Rapids is the Midwest. Cedar Rapids is the Midwest League. You will enjoy the experience.

Dining/Bars/Nightlife

Cedar Rapids has a remarkably surprising selection of international food and **Zins** (227 2nd Ave. SE, Cedar Rapids) for tapas leads the way. Excellent Indian food is available at **Taste of India** (1060 Old Marion Rd., Cedar Rapids). **Village Meat Market & Café** (92 16th Ave. SW, Cedar Rapids) serves a killer Iowa pork tenderloin sandwich. For a taste of the black stuff better known as stout, the **Dublin City Pub** (415 1st St. SE, Cedar Rapids) is Midwest, but Irish through and through.

Hotels/Accommodations

Best Western Plus—90 Twixt Town Rd. NE, Cedar Rapids, IA, 52402, (866) 925-9753
Doubletree Inn—350 First Ave. NE, Cedar Rapids, IA, 52401, (866) 925-9753

CLINTON LUMBERKINGS/
ASHFORD UNIVERSITY FIELD
Midwest League (A) Affiliate of the Seattle Mariners
. . . .

537 Ballpark Dr., Clinton, IA, 52732 / (563) 242-0727

Ashford University Field is an old ballpark that has gotten a few facelifts and constant makeup over the years. The structure was originally constructed in 1937 as a project of the Works Progress Administration (WPA) and is a definite throwback. Clinton is the oldest organization in the Midwest League and their stadium is a virtual museum to the team and league's great past.

While the stadium looks old, the amenities are not. The Clinton organization regularly upgrades portions of the 4,000-seat stadium in order to keep up with the Joneses. After all, competition is thick in Iowa for the Midwest League dollar: there are four teams within just a short distance on the map from each other. Ashford University Field is a portal to the past, but not unkempt. The staff makes sure your entire experience at the ballpark will be top notch.

The food at Ashford University Field is pretty much standard ballpark fare with a dash of barbequed pig here and there. The pulled pork sandwich sets itself apart. It helps being surrounded by some of the best swine in the country. The Leinie's Lumber Lodge in left field offers fans beer choices beyond the corporate labels that dominate ballpark taps these days. Fridays are fish fry nights at Ashford University Field, so grab some lemon and tartar sauce and join in.

SIDE TRIP: VISIT A FIELD OF DREAMS FOR A BUSHEL BASKET OF PERSPECTIVE

The 1989 movie *Field of Dreams* was popular because it was a movie of life that happened to feature baseball. Playing catch with your father was an allegory for spending time with ones you love before they leave you forever. The movie was fiction based on a book by W.P. Kinsella called *Shoeless Joe*, a book about a father, his hero, a son, and how expectations bring us together or pull us apart.

That is why Dyersville is an important stop to blend into any planning you may make for a baseball road trip in Iowa. The house and farm that stood in as Ray and Annie Kinsella's farm in the movie still has the iconic baseball field amid the lush cornfields.

Dyersville is about 35 miles west of Dubuque, 60 miles northwest of Cedar Rapids, and a million miles from your worries. Whether or not you are in need of a dose of perspective, you can find it here. The baseball field serves as a Zen garden on this monastery-like farm. Perfect lines and a field guided by the rules of baseball. Perfect rows and fields guided by the rules of farming. You can walk on a perfect baseball field amid perfect cornfields to consider our imperfect lives.

Take some time and go off the beaten path for a day to see the Field of Dreams in Dyersville, Iowa. Baseball will be there down the road in Davenport, Burlington, Waterloo, or Clinton. Life beckons, so stop and smell the roses, or rather, the freshly mown grass.

Field of Dreams Movie Site—28995 Lansing Rd., Dyersville, IA, 52040, (563) 875-8404

The ballpark is incredibly easy to navigate and the staff make you feel welcome in this classic ballpark in a genteel Mississippi River town. Take in Clinton's Ashford University Field because of the history, flavor, and great people. You will not be disappointed.

 Dining/Bars/Nightlife

The Candlelight Inn (511 Riverview Dr., Clinton) is affordably upscale and an enjoyable experience. There are four locations in Iowa and Illinois. For pizza, locals will point you to **Rastrelli's** (238 Main Ave., Clinton).

For a Midwestern diner experience, try the **Old Town Family Restaurant** (2107 Camanche Ave., Clinton). Your taste buds will not be cheated. **Hump's Midway Bar** (319 S. 2nd St., Clinton) has entered the Clinton sports bar scene and is perfect for pre- or postgame drinks.

 Hotels/Accommodations

Hampton Inn—2781 Wild Rose Cir S., Clinton, IA, 52732, (866) 925-7881

QUAD CITIES RIVER BANDITS/ MODERN WOODMEN PARK

Midwest League (A) Affiliate of the Houston Astros

• •

209 S. Gaines St., Davenport, IA, 52802 / (563) 322-6348

Modern Woodmen Park has one of the most beautiful views in baseball. The Centennial Bridge runs across the Mississippi River just past the first-base/right-field side of the stadium. At night, the bridge is alight, giving fans the feeling that they are watching baseball at a very special ballpark in a great city.

Apparently, others are noticing, too. Modern Woodmen Park was voted the best minor league park in America by 10best.com.

Davenport is one of the four Quad Cities (Rock Island, Moline, and Bettendorf are the others). Davenport has the good fortune of hosting a wonderful organization in the River Bandits. The area is economically vibrant: John Deere and other major corporations call the Quad Cities home. The town comes off as sleepy at times, but this is a bustling region. The folks of the Quad Cities love the River Bandits and love watching baseball in the summer months.

The 7,140-seat stadium was opened in 1931 and stands as a well-kept classic. Strong and sturdy like the people of the Quad Cities, Modern Woodmen Park is a survivor. The worst floods of the century along the Mississippi could not bring down this ballpark treasure in the 1990s. I expect to see this great park around in 2031 to celebrate its 100th birthday.

The concourse of the ballpark is loaded with food options. You do get some unusual fare like the macaroni and cheese smothered hot dog and Carolina nachos featuring pulled pork. But for the most part, Modern Woodmen Park doesn't stray off of the standard ballpark fare path. Though craft beers are a little more abundant at the Good Hops beer stand than most Midwest League ballparks.

If you park at Modern Woodmen, there will be a small fee. However, the club gives a voucher of the same amount to fans as credit at the concession stands. The charge is just to ensure that ticket-holding fans get priority over people looking to poach a free spot in this downtown area.

Once again, what will stand out with your experience at Modern Woodmen Park is the beauty. Beyond the bridge, there will be plaques honoring fans and ballplayers from Quad Cities history. The ballpark is a good walk from along the concourse and the seats are comfortable. The façade is a throwback to another era of the game. This stadium is an experience for fans unto itself. You will have a full ballpark experience at Modern Woodmen Park.

Dining/Bars/Nightlife

I enjoyed a rainy afternoon at **Great River Brewery** (332 E. 2nd St., Davenport) waiting for a game at Modern Woodmen Park. The Organic Farmer Brown Ale was fantastic and they do observe Happy Hour in Iowa ($2.00 a pint). For reasonably priced American fare, try **Barrel House 211** (211 E. 2nd St., Davenport) and take in more of downtown Davenport.

If you are looking to strap on the feedbag, try **The Machine Shed** (7250 Northwest Blvd., Davenport). The Machine Shed's biscuits are as big as your head and you will take home most of your bounty. This is a Mississippi River town and good views of Old Man River can be taken in at **The Boat House** (1201 E. River Dr., Davenport). The deck at The Boat

House is a perfect place to grab a beer and watch the river in Davenport.

Hotels/Accommodations
Radisson Hotel—111 E. 2nd St., Davenport, IA, 52801, (866) 925-1043
Hotel Blackhawk—200 E. 3rd St., Davenport, IA, 52801, (866) 925-7881

BURLINGTON BEES/ COMMUNITY FIELD
Midwest League (A) Affiliate of the Los Angeles Angels
. . . .
2712 Mt Pleasant St., Burlington, IA, 52601 / (319) 754-5705

Burlington is a minor league town straight out of central casting. The small ballpark (3,200 seats) has been around in one form or another since 1947. Burlington is the smallest minor league market to have affiliation in North America. You are in small-town America watching ballplayers who will someday play in one of the biggest cities in the country (Los Angeles).

Community Field is a tight fit and you are not going to get a view of the game when you go to the

concession stand at this classic venue. You will, however, get among one of the finest pork tenderloin sandwiches in baseball (more pork products should be mandated at ballparks in America). The food for the most part, though, is limited to hot dogs, hamburgers, and pizza.

Burlington's ballpark serves the typical menu of corporate beers dashed with some microbrews. However, one beer will stick out: Old Style. Old Style and Old Style Light beer are served at Community Field. Burlington is an enclave of Old Style loyalty and that is good news to fans looking for something beyond the corporate labels.

A game at Community Field will not break the bank, either. The most expensive ticket is less than $10.00 and the prices on the concession stand menu will not rattle you.

Another thing that stands out as a positive to the Community Field ballpark experience is the relative quiet. You are not going to get hit over the head with loud noise or bugged with the constant chatter of wacky sounds or music. The ballpark also does not feel the need to have an on-field contest between every inning to entertain fans.

Sometimes keeping up with your scorecard is just what the doctor ordered at a ballgame.

Community Field is a treat for fans who want an authentic baseball experience without the hassles of traffic jams, noisy P.A. chatter, or having to hand your wallet over at the turnstile.

Dining/Bars/Nightlife

Big Muddy's (710 N. Front St., Burlington) is a riverside joint in a historic building with an extensive menu. If chicken wings are the fix that you need, try **Lips-to-Go** (1000 N. Roosevelt Ave., Burlington).

The pizza at **Moto's Public House** (100 N. 4th St., Burlington) is getting rave reviews along with their vegetarian options. For a drink and American small plates, try **Martini's Grille** (610 N. 4th St., Burlington).

Hotels/Accommodations

Super 8—3001 Kirkwood St., Burlington, IA, 52601, (866) 538-6270
Howard Johnson's—2759 Mount Pleasant St., Burlington, IA, 52601, (866) 573-4235

THE NORTHWOODS LEAGUE

The Northwoods League is a non-affiliated baseball league for college players. The teams are located in Iowa, Minnesota, Michigan, Ontario, and Wisconsin. Most players are "adopted" by local residents and live in spare rooms provided by their adopting family for the summer. Companies who support the teams often provide part-time jobs for players. Many Baseball America top 250 prospects play in the Northwoods League. With some research, you can find a player or two of interest and check them out with a short side trip as part of your planned baseball road trip. Below is a list of Northwoods League teams located in the state of Iowa:

Waterloo Bucks/Riverfront Stadium

850 Park Road, Waterloo, IA, 50703
www.waterloobucks.com

Waterloo's slick 5,100-seat stadium is a jewel in the Northwoods League. It is a worthy stop on any baseball road trip around the state of Iowa. The façade is as quality as any Midwest League ballpark and the amenities within the ballpark make a strong case for Waterloo's status as more than a drive-by ballpark. You should probably take the time to see a game at Riverfront Stadium.

THE AMERICAN ASSOCIATION OF INDEPENDENT PROFESSIONAL BASEBALL

The American Association of Independent Professional Baseball (AAIPB) was founded in 2005 after the Central League collapsed and greater definition came to the independent baseball landscape in North America. The geography of the AAIPB stretches down a central swath of North America from Winnipeg, Saskatchewan, to Amarillo, Texas. Below are teams playing in the American Association of Independent Professional Baseball in Iowa:

Sioux City Explorers/Lewis & Clark Park

3400 Line Dr., Sioux City, IA, 51106
www.xsbaseball.com

Lewis & Clark Park is a good-looking ballpark with a capacity of 3,630. The stadium is befitting of a city the size of Sioux City. Fans who are going around the state would be lucky to see a game if the Explorers are in town, but a drive-by tour and walk around the park would suffice. Sioux City gets high marks for a great design and efficient use of their space.

CHAPTER 4

KENTUCKY

Baseball, Bluegrass,
and Bats

LOUISVILLE SLUGGER FIELD
HOME OF THE LOUISVILLE BATS
AAA Affiliate of the Cincinnati Reds

• •

401 E. Main St., Louisville, KY, 40202
www.batsbaseball.com

Baseball and Louisville have gone together like peas and carrots since the Civil War. Louisville was a member team of the major league version of the American Association in 1882, which merged into the National League in 1892. Unfortunately, this growing rail stop and vital river city fell victim to a pirate in 1899—as in the Pittsburgh Pirates.

Louisville owner Barney Dreyfuss quietly bought controlling interest in the Pittsburgh franchise in 1899. In order to fill his roster, he raided the Louisville Colonels roster and "pirated" 14 players (including future Hall of Famers Honus Wagner and Fred Clarke). Dreyfuss pirated a few other players from around the league, and then folded the Louisville franchise. By 1903, the super roster of mostly one-time Louisville Colonels were playing in the World Series. The media dubbed the Pittsburgh franchise the Pirates and the rest is history.

But a visit to Louisville Slugger Stadium will convince you that the Falls City's baseball fortunes have come back with a vengeance.

Louisville Slugger Stadium is annually being considered for Best Baseball Park in America. The beautiful 13,200-seat facility was configured around the very rail depot that likely serviced the Louisville Colonels as they went off and came home from their road trips. The massive brick building serves as a perfect facade for entry into the ballpark and a year-round entertainment venue. The great hall also shows off the history of Louisville baseball and the many great players who have passed through this city over the past 140 years.

Entertainment is what Louisville Slugger Field is about. The atmosphere is major league with a circus feel: a carousel is even located in the right-field corner of the ballpark. Live bands are a

regular event on Thursday nights to draw folks leaving work from the downtown business district. Themed nights are almost every night at Louisville Slugger Field, so you better be ready for a good time.

And a good time is what Louisville is about. Louisville is home to Churchill Downs and the Kentucky Derby. For two weeks a year, the Derby Festival draws hundreds of thousands to the Falls City for events ranging from the formal to informal. Louisville's drink of choice this time of year is the mint julep, a bourbon, mint, ice, and simple syrup concoction that will leave a reminder of your good times in the form of a hangover. Thankfully, the mint julep is not a formal item at Louisville Slugger Field's concession menu.

Once inside of the ballpark, there is a major league feel. Louisville Slugger Field is configured to feel larger than it actually is in seating. Seating opportunities are available at any point along and above the concourse of the main grandstand. The second level and luxury suites give a higher feel to the ballpark. Seating is available from foul pole to foul pole with affixed seats in left field, grass berms in center, and bleachers in right field. There is no reason a crowd at Louisville Slugger Stadium could not reach 15,000 someday. They certainly have the room to reach that number.

Room and space are big at Louisville Slugger Field, too. The great hall lends itself into spacious concourses that give the fan elbow room on even the most crowded nights. Standing-room-only overlook and patio decks in right field give fans space, but it is a tough fight for comfortable seating. The planners even afforded ample picnic areas outside of the stadium on Jackson St. (first-base side) and Preston St. (third-base side). Inside or outside of the stadium, you will have a perfect level of comfort.

SIDE TRIP: A MUSEUM DEDICATED TO A LOUISVILLE LEGEND

Louisville Slugger is a name as attached to baseball as Babe Ruth, Cy Young, or Cooperstown. This brand of baseball bat has been associated with the game of baseball since the 1870s. Bats are on display throughout the museum used by legendary players from the 1880s through today. You can even see the bat Babe Ruth used to hit his 714th and final home run.

A Louisville Slugger is actually a brand of bat made by Hillerich & Bradsby. The factory that makes the Louisville Slugger bat is on the grounds of the museum. This facility also serves as the corporate headquarters of the company.

Outside of the museum is a 34-ton, 60-plus-foot bat. This marvel, known as the world's largest bat, is truly amazing. Truth is, the massive bat is hollow metal and painted in a wood grain. There are a lot of great displays at the museum beyond the bats like Legos fashioned into major league ballparks and interactive displays for all members of the family to enjoy.

Louisville Slugger Museum—
800 West Main Street, Louisville, 40202—
www.sluggermuseum.com

The food at Louisville Slugger Field is not exceptional, but you can get a bologna sandwich. Yes, a bologna sandwich. It is not the bologna sandwich your mom made. This is a Louisville delicacy. The sandwich is a double stack of two half-inch slices off of a yard-long rind of fresh bologna. The slices are butter grilled, garden dressed, and served on a hearty bun. Comfort food at the ballpark; thank God Louisville has some of the best heart hospitals in America.

Kentucky is a state with underrated barbeque. Louisville Slugger Field has a microbrewery/smokehouse named **Against the Grain** attached to the building. Because of an agreement with the concessionaire, neither food nor beer can be bootlegged into the ballpark. So, enjoy a meal and cop a buzz off of one of a dozen or so taps offered at Against the Grain. Many people hoard tables for hours and hold onto them until the first pitch is thrown, so plan accordingly.

You would be remiss not to venture to downtown Louisville as well. Louisville Slugger Field is a short walk from the downtown center and right by Waterfront Park. Apartment buildings and condominiums targeting young professionals are filling the stadium district, acting as a conduit to the downtown center. Bardstown Road is a short drive or cab ride from this area and full of restaurants, bars, and music venues.

It is completely understandable why Louisville Slugger Field is voted annually among the top-five best minor league ballparks in America.

This brick palace is worthy of the praise. Louisville is a great city with a great baseball tradition. Experience Louisville Slugger Field and see it for yourself. You won't regret the trip.

Dining/Bars/Nightlife

Superchef's Breakfast (2317 Brownsboro Rd., Louisville) in Clifton Heights will thrill your taste buds at breakfast time. You can have an upscale chocolate/lunch experience at **Ghyslain** (721 E. Market St., Louisville). Try not to leave Louisville without getting a classic hot brown, open-face sandwich. The ham and turkey on bread oven-baked in a rue of cheese and topped with bacon was invented at **The Brown Hotel** (335 W. Broadway, Louisville) and is served daily at their restaurant, **J. Graham's Café**.

Louisville has a nightlife that will surprise you. **Sergio's World Beers** (1605 Story Ave., Louisville) is a haven for hopheads, featuring dozens of taps and hundreds of beers. If you want a dive bar without the judgmental hipster vibe, hit **Nachbar** (969 Charles St., Louisville) in the Germantown neighborhood. The **Haymarket Whiskey Bar** (331 E. Market St., Louisville) will give you a taste of top-shelf bourbon from Kentucky's Bourbon Trail at very reasonable prices.

Hotels/Accommodations

Marriott—280 W. Jefferson St., Louisville, KY, 40202, (866) 573-4235
The Brown Hotel—335 W. Broadway, Louisville, KY, 40202, (866) 678-6350
Galt House—140 N. Fourth St., Louisville, KY, 40202, (866) 767-0278

Directions/Transportation/Parking

Downtown Louisville is the connecting point of three major interstates: I-71(from Cincinnati), I-65 (From Indianapolis and Nashville), and I-64 (From St. Louis and Lexington). No matter which way you come from, you will have to get to I-65 to reach Louisville Slugger Field.

From the north on I-65, you will use Exit 136-C (Jefferson St./Downtown). Take the Brook St. ramp to the second right onto Market St. Turn left onto Jackson St., then left onto Main St. The ballpark will be on the right.

From the south on I-65, take Exit 136-B (Brook St.). Keep right and go onto Brook St. Turn right onto Market St. Turn left onto Jackson St., then left onto Main St. The ballpark will be on the right.

Airport: Louisville International Airport (SDF)
Major Airlines: Yes (All major U.S. airlines and Air Canada)
Car Rentals: Yes (Within airport)

BOWLING GREEN HOT RODS/ BOWLING GREEN BALLPARK
Midwest League (A) Affiliate of the Tampa Bay Rays

300 8th Ave., Bowling Green, KY, 42101 / (270) 901-2121

Bowling Green is a relative newcomer to the Midwest League. The stadium itself has only been open since 2009. The organization's roots are in the South Atlantic League: the team was located in Wilmington, North Carolina; Albany, Georgia; and Columbus, Georgia, before settling in Bowling Green, Kentucky. It looks like the team is in Bowling Green and the Midwest League to stay.

Bowling Green is home to the Corvette plant for General Motors and their suppliers (thus, the nickname Hot Rods). The town is in the midst of a 10-year, $150 million revitalization that included the construction of the new ballpark. The business development followed and the city has put together a pretty solid economic zone around the ballpark. Add to that the fact that the people of Bowling Green are some of the

most welcoming in the Midwest League and it will take no time for you to feel comfortable at Bowling Green Ballpark.

Bowling Green Ballpark is an efficient stadium that achieves the goal of being a solid economic development tool. Inside of the ballpark, you find the typical local business signage on the outfield wall that is rampant in the Midwest League. What is more unusual is the unique angles afforded to the outfield wall. Three-hundred-eighteen feet down the left-field line makes for a short porch. A picnic area is above the wall, so watch out if you choose to sit in this area. The design of the ballpark affords for a small second level, but that is only accessible by luxury suite.

The food choices at Bowling Green Ballpark will not amaze you, but the prices are among the most reasonable in minor league baseball. The concourse is good to wander, but the lack of concession stands make for long lines that block the concourse. Tickets are inexpensive and there really isn't a bad seat in the ballpark.

Bowling Green is a beautiful ride down I-65 almost halfway between Louisville and Nashville. The ballpark is a great place to visit if you decide to do the Bourbon Trail after stopping at Cincinnati and Louisville on a five day trip. You will feel welcome on your visit to Bowling Green. Your enjoyable experience at the ballpark will match the hospitality of the people, too.

Dining/Bars/Nightlife

For solid American, stick-to-your-ribs grub, go to **Mariah's** (801 State St., Bowling Green). Locals love the place. For Mexican that stands out from the crowd, try **Garcia's Grill** (1689 Campbell Ln., Bowling Green). Two words: great salsa. **The Home Café & Market Place** (2440 Nashville Rd., Bowling Green) offers a diverse menu with specials that are off of the beaten path. For a good pizza/beer combination, hit the **Mellow Mushroom** (1035 Chestnut St., Bowling Green). The eclectic menu has something for all appetites.

Hotels/Accommodations

Courtyard by Marriott—1010 Wilkinson Trace, Bowling Green, KY, 42103, (866) 925-1043
Hilton Garden Inn—1020 Wilkinson Trace, Bowling Green, KY, 42103, (866) 925-7881
Holiday Inn University Plaza—1021 Wilkinson Trace, Bowling Green, KY, 42103, (866) 925-9753

LEXINGTON LEGENDS/ WHITAKER BANK BALLPARK

South Atlantic League (A) Affiliate of the Kansas City Royals

207 Legends Lane, Lexington, KY, 40505 / (859) 422-RUNS

Lexington is horse country. The people of Lexington live, breathe, and work the horse industry. The horse industry is the top industry in Lexington and it is taken seriously around here. That is why I recommend highly any fan of baseball who loves the beauty of any game to make a visit to **Keeneland Race Track** (4201 Versailles Road, Lexington). A visit to Kenneland is a visit to see how a truly professional, classic horse-racing facility is run.

Of recent, baseball has found its way in a community that prides itself in equine excellence. Whitaker Bank Ballpark is home to the Lexington Legends and a lot of fun. The ballclub has only been around since 2000 and won the South Atlantic League championship right out of the gate in 2001.

The stadium's charming feel is more Southeastern than Midwestern. Fans with special entry tickets can get into a restaurant sponsored by the Kentucky Ale Tap Room before, during, and after the game behind the home-plate area. The stadium is not open concourse, but this area has access to a view of the field. The Budweiser Stables

The Bourbon Trail is proof that God loves Kentucky enough to bless it with perfect streams with limestone beds and enough shade to help make the best bourbon in America. The trip is a must-do for bourbon aficionados and those who want the most beautiful view of horse country, too.

You can mix baseball and bourbon in Kentucky by integrating the Bourbon Trail in any travels between Louisville, Lexington, and Bowling Green. If you look on a map of Kentucky's bourbon country, you will see that it is within a triangle of three major Kentucky cities: Louisville, Frankfort, and Bardstown. The trail has a website (cited below) and there are dozens of small and large bourbon distillers with tasting rooms.

Plus, you get a beautiful drive through the bluegrass hills of Kentucky. Open your car windows at the right time of year and the fragrant mint will provide olfactory bliss. Don't be surprised if you find yourself yearning for a mint julep later that evening after dinner.

Kentucky Bourbon Trail—
www.kybourbontrail.com

and Pepsi Party Deck in right field are perfect for groups of fans looking for the best deal possible. Tickets at Lexington are more expensive than the average minor league ballpark, so budget accordingly.

You will also want to park safely in the ballpark parking lot. The ballpark is in a tougher area of Lexington (I didn't know there was one). The city pegged this area for redevelopment in the early part of the century and things haven't moved as quickly toward that goal as wished. However, it doesn't diminish the experience you will have in the ballpark.

Food-wise, Lexington has done a great job keeping their menu down the middle of the road while incorporating some regional favorites. Personally, I am a fan of Cincinnati chili and Lexington has Gold Star Chili in the house. Beyond the choices at the Kentucky Ale Tap Room and Cincinnati chili, the fare at Lexington is typical ballpark fare.

Whitaker Bank Ballpark does an excellent job integrating the horse farm feel into their design. The colors and the design of the roofs fit the region like a glove. The fans are treated to a lot of entertainment at the ballpark between innings, which differentiates it—in a relaxing way—from the 20 hectic minutes of studying horse bettors are forced to do in between races.

In all, Whitaker Bank Ballpark is a stadium that fits the feel of a community in a town that holds traditions sacred. Baseball is an American tradition that has done well in Lexington. I think we are safe to say it will be around for many years with the help and support of the great fans of Lexington, Kentucky.

 Dining/Bars/Nightlife

Lexington is an international city. Horse industry executives flock in from the Arab Emirates, Ireland, Japan, and Britain daily. So the restaurants have kept pace with the international appeal of the industry in Lexington. Try **Sugano Japanese Restaurant** (1533 Eastland Pkwy. #7, Lexington) for a wide range of Japanese delicacies on their menu. **Masala** (3061 Fieldstone Way, Lexington) is a well-established Indian restaurant that leads the field of great Indian food in Lexington.

For good old-fashioned American fare, try the **Merrick Inn** (1074 Merrick Dr., Lexington). **Guiseppe's Ristorante Italiano** (4456 Nicholasville Rd., Lexington) is a slice of Italy in the middle of Bourbon Country. For a nightcap, go to **Al's Bar** (601 N. Limestone, Lexington). Al's is a hip dive where you can sip Kentucky bourbon with a beer back.

Hotels/Accommodations

Courtyard by Marriott—775 Newtown Ct., Lexington, KY, 40511, (866) 678-6350

Candlewood Suites—603 Ad Color Dr., Lexington, KY, 40511, (866) 767-0278

Residence Inn—1080 Newtown Pike, Lexington, KY, 40511, (866) 925-8676

THE FRONTIER LEAGUE

The Frontier League is a non-affiliated baseball league for college players. The teams are located in Illinois, Kentucky, Missouri, Ohio, and Pennsylvania. The Frontier League even has a traveling team (The Frontier Greys). Most players are "adopted" by local residents and live in spare rooms provided by their adopting family for the summer. Companies who support the teams often provide part-time jobs for players. Many Baseball America top 500 prospects play in the Frontier League. With some research, you can find a player or two of interest and check them out with a short side trip as part of your planned baseball road trip. Below is a list of Frontier League teams located in the state of Kentucky:

Florence Freedom/University of Cincinnati Medical Center Stadium

• •

7950 Freedom Way, Florence, KY, 41042
(859) 594-HITS / www.florencefreedom.com

This 4,200-seat stadium opened in 2004 and is considered among one of the kid-friendliest stadiums in the Frontier League. Fans are given the pleasure of many fireworks nights a year. UCMC Stadium boasts one of the better menus in the league. Florence is within 15 miles of Cincinnati.

CHAPTER 5

MICHIGAN

Pure Baseball,
Great Beaches, and
Good Times

COMERICA PARK
Home of the Detroit Tigers

2100 Woodward Ave., Detroit, MI, 48201
(313) 471-2255 / www.visitdetroit.com

You would be betting good money to say more than half of all Tigers fans were not big fans of leaving old Tiger Stadium. The old girl at "The Corner" of Michigan and Trumbull was a classic with quirks like a second deck in the outfield that hung seven feet over the outfield fence, occasionally turning warning track outs into home runs. The dress she wore was steel and wood decking. Tiger Stadium was gritty and blue collar like its fans.

The change to Comerica Park was met with resistance up and until the ballpark opened. Once inside, Tiger fans adapted to the flashier digs faster than people expected. The design was old-school and that went a long way with the skeptics. What put most Tigers fans over the top was the reverence toward the past inside of the ballpark. Resistance to change tends to wear down when sentimentality is thrown at you by the bushel basket.

Detroit is a founding organization in the American League. The team reeks of history. Their original stadium may have been at "The Corner" since 1895, but this team was so much more than the stadium. Like the Yankees or Red Sox, the Tigers are a sum of all of its parts. Things change and sometimes for the better. Comerica Park is one of those great changes where a great organization doesn't miss a beat.

Up front and to their credit, the Tigers have one of the most affordable ticket price menus in baseball. Ticket prices go from $15.00 in the upper deck to $85.00 in the swankier sections of the lower level. Compare this to Chicago or New York and it looks downright affordable.

A visit to Comerica Park is quickly becoming a must-do for all baseball fans. One thing fans appreciate at Comerica Park is the gracious amount of space they have inside and outside of the ballpark. When you get to the main gate, you will pass through a set of tiger statues before you go into an area on the concourse behind home plate. This plaza-like area that does exactly the opposite of Wrigley Field's main gate: it actually lets you in the stadium without having to deal with a backlog of fans beyond the gate. This may be as good an area for groups and families to find each other as any in baseball. Yes, there are those who want to take pictures with the tiger statues but they will not impede your progress at all.

Back to that whole thing about Tigers fans having a tough time adjusting to change. Beyond the main gate, the first statue you will see is that of the late Ernie Harwell. Tigers fans loved Ernie Harwell— his voice, as well as the history he conveyed nightly to fans calling games at old Tiger Stadium and on road trips all over the American League. Harwell called games for the Tigers from 1960 to 1991, then 1993 to 2002. Ernie was one of them. To know Ernie Harwell and to respect what he stood for within this organization is to know the heart and soul of the Detroit Tigers. These fans are very protective of Ernie and understandably so: he called an incredible game.

The concourse of the ballpark itself is filled with history and fun. If you work the concourse clockwise, you will begin to think you are at the state fair and not a ballpark. A functioning carousel and a working Ferris wheel make up the fairway of rides to entertain children of all ages before, during, and after the game. Once you pass that area, the history of the team begins to pop up in the form of statues.

You'll see well-done statues of Cobb, Kaline, Greenberg, and a few other Tigers greats akin to the statues that grace the concourse at U.S. Cellular Field in Chicago. By the time you absorb this dose of Tigers history, you will be ready to hit your seats and watch some baseball.

The thing that strikes a lot of people I know who have been to Comerica is one thing: the massive green expanse known as the outfield. Old Tiger Stadium had a massive outfield, so the look may

have been worked into the design of Comerica Park as a nod to the old joint. Another thing that strikes fans is the brick red that stands out on the tiers above the left-field concourse. Colors were not in abundance at old Tiger Stadium. Above the green of the grass and the brick red of the walls you get Detroit's skyline. These levels and their colors please the eyes of a fan of aesthetics.

Like the main gate, the massive scoreboard in left field is flanked by guard tigers. No worries: the only animated tiger at the ballpark is Paws, the Detroit Tigers mascot. The only damage Paws can do is squeezing you too hard with a hug. Paws stalks the concourse and stands before and during the game and is always willing to play with the kids.

The food at Comerica Park will make you scratch your head. A piece of Little Caesar's pizza for almost $6.00 (or a pizza for $19.00) when I can walk into one of their stores and take home a whole pizza for $5.00? The food at any specialty stand is pricey at Comerica Park.

Looking at the prices, one can only deduct that the team's payroll is financed by concession sales.

There is a stand operating on the third-base concourse under the Food Network banner that serves an interesting menu. Unfortunately, it is expensive once you get a comparative eye on the concession stands serving basic ballpark fare. A beer and a dog is still $3.00 cheaper than any specialty sandwich served here. Why would you choose to pay more for less? It couldn't be that much better.

One more criticism of the economies of scale for Comerica Park food concessions and I will back off. Detroit is still a blue-collar town. Drop the specialty foods and lower the price of Little Caesar's pizza to Little Caesar's levels. Push more microbrews on top of that and you'll see more Winter's hot dogs and sausages sold. The bacon-wrapped hot dogs move because Tigers fans will eat them. Tigers fans are not looking for specialty sandwiches given the seal of approval of some famous chef. The margins will remain the same or increase. Okay, rant over.

Detroit is a rare American city that has not gone through a sustained renewal. As I am writing this, the city is going through the largest bankruptcy by a city in American history. A manager at the state level is running the city. So, logically (sarcasm alert), the installed city manager and governor approved the construction of a new $450 million publicly financed stadium for the Detroit Red Wings within a week of the bankruptcy filing. This will be the third publicly financed stadium built in Detroit in 15 years.

Detroit has a population of 700,000 and a debt obligation of $20 billion plus. In 1970, the population of Detroit was just over 1.5 million and their government was running a surplus. Whether financing a new hockey stadium makes sense is not for this writer to determine. However, consider this: Detroit's economy is effectively reduced to the automobile industry's executive offices and sports stadiums. If Detroit wants to survive, even grow, investments need to be made in diversifying the economy—not building stadiums for billionaires that can afford to finance their own hobbies.

However, it doesn't mean Detroit and Detroit supporters are not trying. You can find good food in Detroit. You can find a good bar in the stadium district. Unfortunately, the amount of disrepair left behind by the exodus of half of the population in just over three decades. There are solutions to the problems, but the hole for Detroit is deep. Once again, rant over.

A trip to **Greektown** on the People Mover is a good bet for good grub before the game. You can do a head to head test of best coney dog in downtown Detroit between **Lafayette Coney Island** and **American Coney Island**. For barbeque in Detroit, **Slow's BBQ** leads the way. After the game, though, things get sketchy in the downtown area of Detroit. You revel postgame at your own risk in Detroit, especially if it is a night game.

But you are as safe as a kitten at Comerica Park and at any hotels in downtown Detroit. Roaming is a limited thing in Detroit at any time, especially after dark. Be careful and make sure you have access to the phone number of a reputable cab company. However, if you plan your movements well in Detroit, you can have an enjoyable time.

Despite the negative that consumes Detroit these days and the very positive, a trip to Comerica Park is well worth the experience. Tigers fans and ballpark aficionados find something new to enjoy about Comerica Park every time they go back to the place. Almost 2.3 million customers a year since 2000 can't be wrong.

 Ballpark Facts, Figures, & Tips
The tradition of a flagpole on the field was ended after 107 years at Michigan and Trumbull in 2002 when the left-field fence was moved in…The $295 million ballpark was designed by HOKSport/Populous and the Smith Group of Detroit… Israel-born artist Omri Amrany sculpted the statues of the Tigers' greats on the left-field concourse…Owner and Detroit-native Mike Ilitch contributed over $185 million to the construction of Comerica Park…A deal for naming rights with Comerica, a financial services company, yields the Detroit–Wayne County Stadium Authority $2.2 million a year and runs

through 2030… A path is cut from home plate to the pitcher's mound, like early 20th century ballparks, to avoid the wear that comes with conferences on the mound between pitchers and catchers…The Dave Matthews Band played the first event and concert at Comerica Park on July 5, 2000…When the Big 3 automakers went through a rough patch in 2009 and cut back on sponsorship and support for the Tigers, the Tigers responded by hanging a banner that simply said "The Detroit Tigers Support Our Automakers"…Like Wrigley Field, Comerica Park draws flocks of seagulls to its center-field grass. They must be Chet Lemon fans.

Best Tips for Seating

A lot of Tigers fans point to the upper deck as a deal with a great view at Comerica Park. The angle of the seating is not obnoxious and you can pay as little as $15.00 for the experience. If you want an old-school stadium feeling, try the Tiger Den seats. You get a padded individual seat with immediate access to the Tiger Court on the concourse. Wait staff will take your order of the Tiger Court's menu and deliver it directly to your seats. Yes, the price is $85.00 but you would have to pay 10 times that price at Yankee Stadium for the same service level.

There are no obstructed views at Comerica Park. Some people used to joke that Tiger Stadium at Michigan and Trumbull was one big obstructed view. Those days are gone with Comerica Park where the vast bulk of seats have an excellent view.

 Driving Directions/Transportation

Detroit is a car town and public transportation is extremely limited. A car will be needed to do any driving. If you are coming from a hotel, cabs can be found. Also recommended is a GPS: there are a million different ways to get to Comerica Park.

Essentially, you will end up having to find your way to the intersection of I-75 and I-375 no matter where you are coming from in Michigan or Ontario (Windsor). From I-75 North, you will want to exit at the Grand River Ave. (Exit 50) then follow the signs to the ballpark. From I-75 South, you will want to exit at the Mack Ave. exit (Exit 52) then follow signs to the ballpark.

Parking

You will pay anywhere from $10.00 to $25.00 for surface and garage parking around Comerica Park. Of course, the closer you get and the more secure the garage, the more expensive the parking. The Tigers do own a number of garages attached and adjacent to the ballpark and parking there can be purchased in advance for $10.00 to $13.00.

Airport: Detroit Metropolitan Wayne County Airport **(DTW)**

Car Rentals

Advantage - (800) 367-2277
Alamo/Vanguard - (800) 327-9633
Avis - (800) 331-1212
Budget - (800) 527-0700
Dollar - (800) 421-6878
Enterprise - (800) 325-8007
Hertz - (800) 654-3131
National /Vanguard - (800) 227-7368

Dining/Bars/Nightlife

Roast (1128 Washington Ave., Detroit) is a Detroit steak house that can stand up against any in the country when it comes to quality and service. Once again, for the best barbeque in the city, hit **Slow's BBQ** (2138 Michigan Ave., Detroit). The pulled chicken sandwich ranks among the best sandwiches in North America.

Detroit is a Coney Island hot dog town. Coneys have competitively co-existed at **American Coney Island** (115 Michigan Ave., Detroit) and **Lafayette Coney Island** (118 W. Lafayette Blvd., Detroit) for decades. The restaurants are within feet of each other. However, **Zeff's Coney Island** (2469 Russell St., Detroit) is giving both of them a run for their money and winning more and more fans every day.

For a beer before or after the game, try **Jacoby's German Biergarten** (624 Brush St., Detroit). You can run into a bar with old-world character at the **Park Inn at Bucharest Grill** (2040 Park Ave., Detroit). **Foran's Grand Trunk Pub** (612 Woodward Ave., Detroit) has a classic facade and interior wooden bar giving guests a view of Detroit's great architectural history.

Hotels/Accommodations

Hilton Garden Inn—351 Gratiot Ave., Detroit, MI, 48226, (866) 573-4235

Greektown Casino—1200 Saint Antoine St., Detroit, MI, 48226, (866) 678-6350

The Atheneum—1000 Brush Ave., Detroit, MI, 48226, (866) 767-0278

The Westin—1114 Washington Blvd., Detroit, MI, 48226, (866) 925-4159

Holiday Inn Express—1020 Washington Blvd., Detroit, MI, 48226, (866) 925-8676

MGM Grand—1777 3rd St., Detroit, MI, 48226, (866) 538-0251

Doubletree Suites—525 West Lafayette Blvd., Detroit, MI, 48226, (866) 538-1314

Courtyard by Marriott—333 E. Jefferson Ave., Detroit, MI, 48226, (866) 538-6252

Crowne Plaza—2 Washington Blvd., Detroit, MI, 48226, (866) 538-9298

Motor City Casino—2901 Grand River Ave., Detroit, MI, 48201, (866) 539-5067

Ballpark/Neighborhood Security

Security at Comerica Park is very good for regular season games and extremely heightened when the Tigers are in the playoffs. Greater Detroit has its crime and public safety response problems. The response times for 911 calls averaged 58 minutes in Detroit according to a July 2013 *New York Times* report. Residents have privately coordinated emergency response plans on their own considering this reality. As a visitor, you should do the same. Be very engaged with your concierge or host family. Keep the phone number of a reliable cab company on you at all times. Avoid being out too late. Detroit is a city where you can have fun, but be very cautious. Take these precautions and you will enjoy your experience at Comerica Park in Detroit.

GREAT LAKE LOONS/DOW DIAMOND
Midwest League (A) Affiliate of the
Los Angeles Dodgers

· ·

825 East Main Street, Midland, MI, 48640

Midland, Michigan, is a company town. Dow Chemical and the community rallied their resources to build this 5,300-seat ballpark called Dow Diamond in 2007. Dow Chemical donated the land, the

Dow plant is in the distance beyond the fence, and the ballpark dons the corporate name of the town's biggest company.

Dow Diamond is a ballpark built for the comfort of the fan. Knowing that April and late August will be cool, fire pits and fireplaces have been installed on the concourse. The generous roof gives cover to a good portion of the main grandstand. Lawn seating wraps around the ballpark from just beyond first base through right field and to the left-field pole. A concourse called the Northern Lights Pavilion dominates the concourse along the left-field line.

You have room to get around at Dow Diamond. The concourse is continuous around the field and a nice way to get in a walk before the game. The scoreboard in right field is massive and clear as a bell and easy on the fan's eyes. You will see two indistinguishable mascots

on your walk. To clarify, the taller mascot is Rall E. Camel and the bird-like mascot is Lou E. Loon. The kids will love them.

You won't get much more than the standard food a ballpark can offer at Dow Diamond. The beer list is not that exciting, either. However, Dow Diamond is a nice ballpark and you should have an overall good baseball experience.

 ### Dining/Bars/Nightlife

Midland is a corporate town and where there is commerce, there is usually better than average food. American fare is offered at **Diamond Jim's** (101 E. Main St., Midland) in downtown Midland that would rival anything a big city could offer. For stick-to-your-ribs, smoked delights, head to **Bone**

Daddy's BBQ (3216 Bay City Rd., Midland). You won't leave hungry from either place. **Whine** (337 E. Wackerly St., Midland) is a tapas/small plate bar that stands out from the pack. The great thing about tapas is that you can mix and match the sweet and savory to match the great wine or sangria you have ordered. Whine excels at both food and drink.

Hotels/Accommodations

Spring Hill Suites—800 Joe Mann Blvd., Midland, MI, 48642, (866) 573-4235

Residence Inn—850 Joe Mann Blvd., Midland, MI, 48642, (866) 678-6350

Holiday Inn—810 Cinema Dr., Midland, MI, 48642, (866) 925-8676

LANSING LUGNUTS/
COOLEY LAW SCHOOL STADIUM

Midwest League (A) Affiliate of the Toronto Blue Jays

505 E. Michigan Ave., Lansing, MI, 48912

The ownership of the Lansing Lugnuts is in the entertainment business, for sure. The capital city of Michigan is home to one of the biggest ballparks in the Midwest (11,000 seats) and what is likely the best menu in minor league baseball. This is a great ballpark for a great community.

Cooley Law School Stadium has a great history of being among the most accessible ballparks in America. The Lansing Lugnuts should take pride in their constant updates to make the stadium more accessible for the disabled. Baseball is the American game and Lansing is proving that inclusion is an American virtue that can pay dividends.

The ballpark is below grade and the view from any seat is great. The concourse is a complete circle around the ballpark and the team uses the area for more than just concessions. On theme nights like Bark in the Park, pet stores and adoption agencies are able to set up kiosks and pedal their respective products. Family days have a carnival-like atmosphere and the occasional superhero night comes off like a miniature version of Comic-Con. The Lansing Lugnuts engage with their fans. That is why the Cooley Law School Stadium turnstiles are constantly spinning.

Want a pickle? Pickles are offered at most concession stands for a buck. Yes, this is the home of the foot-long fish taco. Cheesesteaks at Cooley Law School Stadium get thumbs up from the Lugnuts fans. You are not inundated with standard ballpark fare from concession stand to concession stand at Cooley Law School Stadium. You can get some really good barbeque at this ballpark for next to nothing: a half a rack of ribs and their pulled pork sandwich are at a price point that will make you think you are getting away with something.

Because of their team affiliation with Toronto, LaBatt beer is offered. Besides the presence of Leinenkugel's craft products, you are pretty much exposed to offerings from the larger U.S. brewers.

The Lansing Lugnuts understand the very basic premise that in order for fans to spend money inside the ballpark they first must be able to afford the ticket. Tickets at Cooley Law School Stadium range from $8.00 to $11.00. Parking, ticket, a hot dog, and a beer for just over $25.00 is a deal, but I bet you spend more. The team store has among the largest and most innovative products in minor league baseball.

Cooley Law School Stadium is a prerequisite for fans who seek out great ballpark experiences. This ballpark ranks among one of the best deals in baseball for the dollar you are spending. Take a road trip to Lansing and find out why fans are raving about Cooley Law School Stadium.

Dining/Bars/Nightlife

Golden Harvest Restaurant (1625 Turner St., Lansing) serves a hearty diner menu while maintaining high quality. The most reputable Italian joint in Lansing these days is **DeLuca's** (2006 W. Willow St., Lansing) where you will have to wait to dine in, so consider calling for carry-out. Parking can sometimes be a hassle at DeLuca's.

The **EagleMonk Pub & Brewery** (4906 W. Mount Hope, Lansing) is a solid microbrewery for this university town and state capital. Locals and travelers alike give high marks to **Stober's Bar** (812 E. Michigan Ave., Lansing) for atmosphere—plus, they have shuffleboard.

Hotels/Accommodations

Radisson—111 N. Grand Ave., Lansing, MI, 48933, (866) 573-4235
Quality Inn—3121 E. Grand River Ave., Lansing, MI, 48912, (866) 678-6350
Courtyard by Marriott—2710 Lake Lansing Rd., Lansing, MI, 48912, (866) 767-0278

WEST MICHIGAN WHITECAPS/ FIFTH THIRD BALLPARK

Midwest League (A) Affiliate of the Detroit Tigers

4500 West River Drive, Comstock Park, MI, 49321

Grand Rapids is an economically diverse community that sits just 25 miles inland from Lake Michigan. It is home to major retailer grocer Meijer and carpet cleaning giant Bissell. When the people of Grand Rapids want to unwind after work, Fifth Third Ballpark in Comstock Park is just what the doctor ordered.

Fifth Third Ballpark in Grand Rapids is a lot like the Fifth Third Bank Ballpark of fellow Midwest League member, the Kane County Cougars. Built high on a hill, the stadium is mainly a grandstand bowl with luxury suites. The outfield, like Kane County, has group-outing patios. One big difference is the concourse of Grand Rapids' Fifth Third Ballpark encircles the whole ballpark.

Oh, and the ballpark in Grand Rapids has a staging area for people who want to eat a fully loaded four-pound cheeseburger that has almost 4,900 calories and 300 grams of fat. That is five days of your recommended daily allowance of fat. When it comes to food, the menu at Fifth Third Ballpark seems like a challenge from top to bottom. Stick to the foods that will not put you in the cardiac ward at the nearest hospital and avoid the challenge. Your spouse will thank you on the way home.

One feature that sticks out at this very functional stadium is a beautiful waterfall beyond the third-base area. The walk along the concourse is made more enjoyable by this natural feature. The concourse itself is very spacious and the signage is very accommodating. The scoreboard is not the most impressive, but it does the job.

Grand Rapids is a very comfortable community and their fans come out consistently for the West Michigan Nine. Take your time and drive along the Lake Michigan coastline before veering off to Highway 196. Lake Michigan is a national treasure you will not regret taking in while you are in this area of the world. You also won't regret taking in a game at Fifth Third Ballpark.

SIDE TRIP: MICHIGAN WEST COAST BEACH TOWNS—
A MIDWEST SUMMER'S DREAM

Grand Rapids is a great starting point for a journey down the western coast of Michigan to see some of the best beach towns America can offer. Michigan has the most coastline of any state in the union (yep, think about it). A drive down Highway 31 to Highway 196 features six great beach destinations that have made Lake Michigan a great vacation spot for Midwest families and friends for generations.

First, you will drive out of Grand Rapids down to Grand Haven. Grand Haven is consistently rated in the top 10 beaches in America on a yearly basis by travel industry list makers. The warm beaches, a 2.5 mile boardwalk, and entertainment options ranging from fishing to art galleries will keep you occupied through your stay.

Moving south from Grand Haven, you will hit Holland. Holland has its windmills, tulips, and world renowned Tulip Festival. However, Holland is anything but wooden shoes in summer. The beach community comes alive with street performers and farmer's markets.

One of the fastest growing areas of Michigan is Saugatuck-Douglas. The property here is hot because artists have made this area home for decades and built a micro-economy focused on art, food, and the finer parts of life. Saugatuck has become somewhat of a go-to place for East and West Coast property seekers who want water, quiet, and Midwestern charm without giving up modern conveniences. An easy 10-minute inland from Saugatuck on Route 89 takes you to Fennville for Crane's for killer fruit pies, incredible art, and the Salt of the Earth restaurant.

A drive southward on the Red Arrow Highway (Route 12) from Saugatuck will present you South Haven. Quaint farm stands dot the road in this area featuring Michigan peaches and blueberries. You'll stop for sure. The pier and lighthouse boldly jut out in black and red against the beige sands of South Haven Beach. The Harbor of South Haven is a great place to take in a sunset and a glass of red from local vintners Round Barn or St. Julian.

Tucked in the southwest corner of Michigan is the Harbor Country, home to New Buffalo. People here love their summer: the beach all day and ice cream at night. A killer cheeseburger can be found at Redamak's on Route 12. Families and groups of friends will love the rooftop bar at the Stray Dog Bar & Grill.

West Michigan Beach Towns Information: www.beachtowns.org

Dining/Bars/Nightlife

San Chez (38 Fulton St. W., Grand Rapids) is a tapas bar that makes the service of small plates a culinary art. If you are in Grand Rapids for business, **The Chop House** (190 Monroe Ave. N.W., Grand Rapids) is a good excuse for an excellent meal with clients or co-workers.

Grand Rapids is a good beer town and the microbreweries **HopCat** (25 Ionia Ave S.W., Grand Rapids), the **Grand Rapids Brewing Company** (1 Ionia Ave S.W., Grand Rapids), and **Founders Brewing** (235 Grandville Ave. S.W, Grand Rapids) are known throughout the Midwest.

Hotels/Accommodations

Travelodge—65 28th St. S.W., Grand Rapids, MI, 49548, (866) 678-6350
Amway Grand Plaza—187 Monroe Ave N.W., Grand Rapids, MI, 49503, (866) 573-4235

THE FRONTIER LEAGUE

The Frontier League is a non-affiliated baseball league for college players. The teams are located in Illinois, Kentucky, Missouri, Ohio, and Pennsylvania. The Frontier League even has a traveling team (The Frontier Greys). Most players are "adopted" by local residents and live in spare rooms provided by their adopting family for the summer. Companies who support the teams often provide part-time jobs for players. Many Baseball America top 500 prospects play in the Frontier League. With some research, you can find a player or two of interest and check them out with a short side trip as part of your planned baseball road trip. Below is a list of Frontier League teams located in the state of Michigan:

Traverse City Beach Bums/Wuerfel Park
· ·
333 Stadium Drive, Traverse City, MI, 49685
www.traversecitybeachbums.com

The people of Traverse City love their Beach Bums. The 3,520-seat stadium itself looks like a set of resort condominiums standing side by side. But the ballpark works and the team and community make every game as comfortable as a day at the beach. This ballpark is among the most impressive structures for the Frontier League.

THE NORTHWOODS LEAGUE

The Northwoods League is a non-affiliated baseball league for college players. The teams are located in Iowa, Minnesota, Michigan, Ontario, and Wisconsin. Most players are "adopted" by local residents and live in spare rooms provided by their adopting family for the summer. Companies who support the teams often provide part-time jobs for players. Many Baseball America top 250 prospects play in the Northwoods League. With some research, you can find a player or two of interest and check them out with a short side trip as part of your planned baseball road trip. Below is a list of Northwoods League teams located in the state of Michigan:

Battle Creek Bombers/C.O. Brown Stadium

1392 Capital Ave NE, Battle Creek, MI, 49017
www.battlecreekbombers.com

Opened in 1991, Battle Creek has been home to semi-professional and minor league baseball since opening the ballpark. The ballpark is an impressive structure that hosts events beyond baseball. The 4,701-seat stadium and the Bombers organization are setting standards in the Northwoods League.

Kalamazoo Growlers (2014–New Franchise)/ Homer Stryker Field

251 Mills Street, Kalamazoo, MI, 49048
www.northwoodsleague.com/kalamazoo

Homer Stryker Field was home to the Kalamazoo Kings of the Frontier League until the team folded in 2011. The ownership of the Battle Creek franchise has purchased a stake in the new Kalamazoo franchise of the Northwoods League. The 4,000-seat ballpark built in 1963 will be re-opening for baseball operations in 2014.

SIDE TRIP: BELL'S BEER AND NEW BASEBALL IN K'ZOO

Kalamazoo is welcoming back baseball in 2014 by joining Battle Creek as a Michigan franchise in the independent Northwoods League. The Kalamazoo Kings played at Homer Stryker Field in the Frontier League from 2001 to 2011.

A stop at Stryker Field for a ballgame should be accompanied by a trip to Bell's Brewery in Kalamazoo. Owner/rebel Larry Bell is a brewer's brewer and a fan of the beer drinker and the home brewer. Four tours are run each Saturday and three tours each Sunday. Lunch and incredible beer can be enjoyed in the aptly named Eccentric Café. Diners can get appetizers to main plates of some of the best foods to pair with their diverse menu of beers. The General Store up front sells home brewer supplies and even provides novice brewers recommendations.

Bell's Brewery—355 E. Kalamazoo Ave., Kalamazoo, MI — Open seven days a week.

CHAPTER 6

MINNESOTA

Beautiful Ballparks
and an
Independent Spirit

TARGET FIELD
Home of the Minnesota Twins

. . . .

1 Twins Way, Minneapolis, 55403
(800) 33-TWINS / www.minneapolis.org

> "Target Field looks to be the Eighth Wonder of the World, a
> temple on the order of Wrigley or Fenway or the Acropolis, a
> beautiful little bandbox of a ballpark tucked snugly into the
> streets of old warehouses and the Burlington rail yards, with
> commuter trains running to its front door, a sight that fills me
> with unmitigated dizzy delight."
> —*Garrison Keillor, Writer/Humorist/Twins Fan*

The people of Minneapolis and St. Paul love their Twins. They also
like the rare Minnesota event called a summer day. Too bad they
had to spend almost 30 years playing in a domed stadium. The
discussion of a new ballpark in the Twin Cities started at the turn of
the century. Things got so contentious that the commissioner included
the Twins in a plan for contracting teams because the city would not
resolve the stadium issue. It is funny how the threat of contraction
got new stadium plans passed in three of the four threatened cities
(Minneapolis, Miami, and Montreal/Washington. Tampa Bay is still
working on a financing plan). In April 2010, the Minnesota Twins
moved into Target Field after a 10-year battle over financing between
the taxpayers and the Twins ownership.

The taxpayers of Minnesota were on the hook for $350 million and
the organization shelled out $130 million. Target pitched in a long-
term deal for naming rights and the die was cast. Outdoor baseball
was back in Minnesota for the first time since the Twins played in
Metropolitan Stadium in 1980.

To tell you how beautiful Target Field is, read the quote again at
the head of the chapter by Garrison Keillor. Take a breath, consider
his lofty words, and realize this: Mr. Keillor was among the biggest
opponents of public financing for the stadium. Keillor may still be

against public financing of the stadium, but he is a fan of Target Field.

In April 2010, the hip Warehouse District of Minneapolis welcomed its newest neighbor, Target Field. The limestone structure is a piece of art that blends in well with the immediate area. The roof of the stadium provides more than ample shade for the regular sell-out crowds that fill Target Field. Target Plaza is considered the main attraction where families and groups meet before going toward the interesting gate system of the stadium. After you pass a massive piece of art in the shape of a baseball glove and the old foul pole from Metropolitan Stadium, you will be led toward gates named after Twins greats Harmon Killebrew, Tony Oliva, Rod Carew, and Kirby Puckett. The next thing you will see is among one of the most beautiful ballparks you have ever seen.

At just about 40,000 seats, Target Field does a lot of good with the room it is given. The bulk of the seats are in the lower rung, from foul pole to foul pole. The decks are deceiving because they are not traditional decks, but what used to be called loges (two sections on top of each other that share a concourse). The luxury suites blend in as unassuming because of the limestone palate. The bleachers in right and left field are not uncomfortable bleachers, but seats with a ton of common areas (including fire pits for colder evenings).

The natural effect of Target Field is pure Minnesota. The softness of the gray metal against the limestone which cradles the stadium's green seats says Northwoods comfort. The flow of the crowd on the concourse is good even on days with standing-room-only crowds. Target Field is efficient and sophisticated; a worldly stadium that blends into its humble surroundings.

Every inch of this stadium is used to benefit the fan. Small nooks like the Legends Club Lounge or the Met Club on the club level are open to all season ticket holders. These special clubs serve as a reward for loyalty through the years. Special areas were built for all fans in appreciation of their support, like the Twins Ballpark Tavern. Art installations are everywhere at Target Field, further increasing the stadium's uniqueness.

You will not go hungry at Target Field and your choices are plentiful on the menu. Excellent Mexican can be found at Senor Smokes (sections 105 and 305). The Hennepin Grille offers all grilled and smoked encased meats Minnesotans love at a ball game. So loved is the Minnesota State Fair that Target Field has a State Fair stand on the center-field concourse that serves the best of fairway foods. Frankie V's honors Twins pitching great Frank Viola with Italian food stands in the Legend's Club and sections 122 and 319. The butter-fat content in the ice cream offered at the Creamery would make even the heartiest Wisconsinite blush.

The choice of beer at Minnesota is extensive compared to most major league ballparks. The large brewer choices are offered at almost every concession stand. Breweries like nearby Summit, Surly, and Leinenkugel offer multiple labels to fans. Minnesota classics like Grainbelt and Schell's grace the menus at Target Field as they did the Metrodome and Metropolitan Stadium.

Don't worry about missing any of the game as you grab food and drink: architect Populous designed the most deceivingly spacious concourses in baseball that view the field at every point of the lower level. You will not be inundated with artificial sound every second of the game, which is nice in this day and age of constant chatter at ballparks. Pray for a Twins home run because the main scoreboard featuring the old-school Twins logo from the Metropolitan Stadium days lights up like a Christmas tree.

Because of the struggle to get this gem of a stadium largely financed by taxpayer support? Free viewing access. Knotholes have been built into the ballpark plaza and fans strolling by the ballpark can comfortably come and go from these viewing areas. Odds are, they will get a look and see that the view is much better from inside and hit the ticket booth for a reasonably priced ticket.

The Twins have a Majestic Team Store attached to the Target Plaza that doesn't connect to the ballpark, but fans can get an eye on the game as they shop. The store is within the effective flow of Target Plaza as you come and go from the game.

Getting to and from the game at Target Field is easy by car: the stadium has over 20,000 parking spots available to fans. Target Field is also on the city's light rail line. The exit for the light rail line is in the left-field corner. Getting in and out of the stadium zone is not going to be a difficult task.

Target Field is a winner for Twins fans and visitors who road trip to the Twin Cities to marvel at its beauty. Take a plane, take a train, or drive your car…just get to Minneapolis to see this comfortably beautiful "wonder" of a ballpark in an incredibly welcoming city.

Ballpark Facts, Figures, & Tips

The Minnesota Twins are a franchise who has always had to share a stadium with other franchises in the Twin Cities. Target Field is the first ballpark dedicated solely to baseball in their history…If you are attending an early season game and wondering how the grass on the field is so green, the high-quality turf is heated year-round with a heating grid that never lets the roots get below 40 degrees…While the scoreboard/video screen is among the largest in the major leagues, the actual property the stadium is on is the smallest patch of land in the major leagues (only 8.6 acres)…Twins fans now have fewer than half of the upper deck seats they had at the Metrodome and could not be more thankful for the architect's kind gesture…In the upper deck, special heating devices are employed to keep fans as comfortable as possible in April and September…The 54 luxury suites blend into the general design of the stadium very well, making them almost indistinguishable from the other levels of the ballpark…The limestone used in building Target Field is all Minnesota limestone…The Twins sparingly retire uniform numbers. The six numbers retired by the Twins are Blyleven (28), Carew (29), Hrbek (14), Killebrew (3), Oliva (6), and Puckett (34)…Target Field advertises that they have the most legroom of any seats in baseball…Ladies rejoice: the ratio of restrooms is 60 percent to 40 percent women's restrooms to men's restrooms at Target Field…

You can also find statues dedicated to former owner Calvin Griffith and Kent Hrbek at Target Field…Shares the distinction of being one of two LEED certified ballparks in Major League Baseball (Washington's Nationals Park is the other)…Awarded "Sports Facility of the Year" by *Sports Business Daily* in 2011 and "Best Stadium Experience" by ESPN in 2010.

Best Tips for Seating

Twins games at Target Field are a tough ticket to wrangle. Attendance records were being tested the first two years of the new ballpark's existence, but demand at Target Field has fallen to a still-strong 85 percent to 90 percent. The 2014 All-Star Game is at Target Field and season-ticket holders will have first dibs, further cutting down the availability of tickets. To purchase tickets on the day of game can sometimes prove to be a tough task, so follow the motto of "consilium in progressus" (Latin for "plan in advance").

A lot of Target Field regulars tout the seats in the lower concourse from first base to third base because of the closeness to the action. Some of the best deals in the ballpark appear to be in the outfield from foul pole to foul pole, though. You have access to the entire vibrant concourse and great views of the field. The upper levels are not obnoxiously angled to induce vertigo and are comfortable.

Many fans have advised that one should throw away the notion of "Minnesota nice" when attending a game at Target Field. "Minnesota nice" is a term applicable to Minnesotans who will welcome you with open arms and genuinely appreciate your presence. "Minnesota nice" exists at Target Field…unless you root for the other team. This isn't a Minnesota-only thing, but definitely a Midwest thing. However, it tends to be more apparent at Target Field because Minnesotans have a general reputation for being among the nicest people in the world…unless you root for the other team.

Driving Directions/Transportation

From the east or northwest of the metropolitan area, you will want to take I-94 into the city and exit on Highway 55 (Olson Memorial Hwy.). You will want to turn right/east after exiting then another right at North 7th St./Hwy. 55. Target Field will be in your sights at that point.

From the west or southwest of the metropolitan area, you want to take I-394 and exit at 6th St. North or 4th St. North. This will put you in an area with great parking options and a short walk from the ballpark.

From the north of the metropolitan area, take I-35 into the city until you reach the divide of the highway. You will choose I-35 West at this point. Drive until you merge onto I-94 West and exit at Highway 55 (Olson Memorial Hwy.). You will want to turn right/east after exiting then another right at North 7th St./Hwy. 55. Target Field will be in your sights at that point.

From the south of the metropolitan area, take I-35 into the city until you reach the divide of the highway. You will choose I-35 West at this point. Exit at either 5th Ave. South or 7th Ave. South. Target Field is just beyond the stadium complex that includes the Target Center. Parking is abundant in this area.

Parking

The planners of Target Field found the best area of the city to plan a stadium complex because a lot of parking is in this area. The immediate area around the stadium has 20,000 parking spaces. You will not have a hard time finding parking at a reasonable price when you visit Target Field.

Airport: Minneapolis–St. Paul International Airport (MSP)

Car Rentals
Advantage - (800) 777-5500

Alamo - (800) 327-9633
Avis - (800) 831-2847
Budget - (800) 527-0700
Dollar - (800) 800-4000
Enterprise - (800) 325-8007
Hertz - (800) 654-3131
National - (800) 227-7368
Thrifty - (800) 847-4389

Dining/Bars/Nightlife

Minneapolis–St. Paul is no longer about lutefisk, Swedish meatballs, and lingenberries. This metropolitan area has evolved into a vital foodie destination and the music/bar scene is among the best in North America. You will neither starve nor have a bad time on the town in the Twin Cities.

The Bachelor Farmer (50 N. 2nd Ave., Minneapolis) is building a reputation as a hot spot for new American cuisine with a Scandinavian influence. You can grab a Juicy Lucy—a Minnesota delicacy where the cheese is cooked into the middle of the hamburger—at **Cuzzy's Bar & Grill** (507 Washington Ave N., Minneapolis).

Ike's Food & Cocktails (50 S. 6th St., Minneapolis) has a solid menu of mostly American fare for brunch, lunch, and dinner. The praise for **112 Eatery** (112 N. 3rd St., Minneapolis) is all about the quality of the food at this downtown joint. Try the sobe noodles or the burger if you want a small taste of 112's massive menu of solid choices.

You can feel authentically Irish even if you aren't from the Emerald Isle at **Kieran's Irish Pub** (600 Hennepin Ave., Minneapolis). Prince, Semisonic, and Soul Asylum got their respective starts at places like **First Avenue** (701 1st Ave. N., Minneapolis) near downtown.

Hotels/Accommodations

Minneapolis–St. Paul is a major city with major options when it comes to hotels. The diverse economy of the area makes it corporate headquarters for hundreds of major national and regional companies, which improves the quality of the hotel stock. Below is a list of hotels in the Twin Cities near Target Field with good to excellent reputations:

Marriott City Center—30 S. 7th St., Minneapolis, MN, 55402, (866) 925-7881

Radisson—35 S. 7th St., Minneapolis, MN, 55402, (866) 925-9753

Residence Inn—45 S. 8th St. Minneapolis, MN, 55402, (866) 538-0154

The Westin—88 S. 6th St., Minneapolis, MN, 55402, (866) 538-0293

The Marquette Hilton—710 Marquette Ave., Minneapolis, MN, 55402, (866) 538-1349

W—The Foshay—821 Marquette Ave., Minneapolis, MN, 55402, (866) 538-6270

The Grand Hotel—615 Second Avenue S., Minneapolis, MN, 55402, (866) 538-9334

Crowne Plaza—618 2nd Ave. S., Minneapolis, MN, 55402, (866) 539-5072

The Depot Renaissance—225 3rd Ave. S., Minneapolis, MN, 55401, (866) 582-9492

Hotel Ivy—201 S. 11th St., Minneapolis, MN, 55403, (866) 712-4780

Ballpark/Neighborhood Security

The Minnesota Twins organization has worked with the city of Minnesota to create one of the most proactive security plans for Target Field and downtown Minneapolis for Twins games. This doesn't mean crime never happens, it just means the local authorities have worked to mitigate crime in and around Target Field. Nothing is absolute, but Minnesota and Target

Field provide one of the safest atmospheres to watch and enjoy baseball.

THE NORTHWOODS LEAGUE

The Northwoods League is a non-affiliated baseball league for college players. The teams are located in Iowa, Minnesota, Michigan, Ontario, and Wisconsin. Most players are "adopted" by local residents and live in spare rooms provided by their adopting family for the summer. Companies who support the teams often provide part-time jobs for players. Many Baseball America top 250 prospects play in the Northwoods League. With some research, you can find a player or two of interest and check them out with a short side trip as part of your planned baseball road trip. Below is a list of Northwoods League teams located in the state of Minnesota:

Alexandria Blue Anchors/Knute Nelson Memorial Park

503 5th Ave. W., Alexandria, MN, 56308
www.blueanchors.com

This 1,500-seat stadium was built back in 1938 and retains a lot of the old-school charm of a classic ballpark. The Blue Anchors (previously the Beetles) draw smaller-than-average crowds, so tickets can be found to see this mainly wooden throwback.

Duluth Huskies/Wade Stadium

101 N. 35th Ave. W., Duluth, MN, 55807
www.duluthhuskies2.com

Duluth's 4,200-seat ballpark was built in the early 1940s when Duluth was an emerging city in the metals industry. Duluth was an NFL city at one point (the Duluth Kelleys, aka, the Eskimos, 1923–25) and could have been what Green Bay is today if Mr. Halas had pointed his loan money to Duluth and not Green Bay. You must see this Works Progress Administration stadium before it goes away. It's nice to see a classic ballpark from a classic era in an old-school town.

Mankato Moondogs/Franklin Rogers Park

601 Reed St., Mankato, MN, 56001
www.mankatomoondogs.com

Mankato's 1,400-seat ballpark was opened in 1961 and has hosted the Northwoods League team since 1999. The simple grandstand with the generous roof is a perfect setting for a Northwoods League organization.

Rochester Honkers/Mayo Field

403 E. Center St., Rochester, MN, 55904
www.rochesterhonkers.com

Rochester is home to the Mayo Clinic and a vital part of the entire Minnesota economy. This simple ballpark caters to a Honkers after-work crowd usually coming from medical industry. The 2,570-seat stadium has a comfortable grandstand with a great roof. Beware of obstructed views.

St. Cloud Rox/Joe Faber Field

5001 Veterans Drive, St. Cloud, MN, 56303
www.stcloudrox.com

This simply classic 2,000-seat stadium has a welcoming facade for fans and is among one of the top draws in the Northwoods League. St. Cloud is a hockey town with an appreciation for what little summer they get, so a night at the ballpark is a welcome event for the local residents.

Willmar Stingers/Bill Taunton Stadium

1401 S.W. 22nd St., Willmar, MN, 56201
www.willmarstingers.com

Willmar is becoming a place where talent goes to play in the Northwoods League. A good count of their alumni can be found in the major leagues. This simple ballpark has room for 1,500 people and the seating is evenly divided between armchairs and bleachers. The roof provides ample shade on the rare hot day in the Willmar Lakes region.

SIDE TRIP: VISIT "MOONLIGHT" GRAHAM IN CHISHOLM, MINNESOTA

The name Archibald "Moonlight" Graham became known to baseball fans and film lovers in the movie *Field of Dreams* with Kevin Costner, James Earl Jones, and Amy Madigan. After working through Class B ball, Graham made the roster of the mighty New York Giants in June of 1905. Graham played defense in the bottom of the eighth inning only to get stranded on deck in the ninth as the game ended in a rare loss for the Giants.

Moonlight earned his medical degree after playing ball. As the movie indicates, the greater tragedy would have been if Moonlight, now "Doc" Graham, had never been a doctor. He served Chisholm, Minnesota, as a family doctor for 50 years and was every bit the good person played by Burt Lancaster in the 1989 movie. Scenes of James Earl Jones' character researching "Doc" Graham were directly taken from author W.P. Kinsella's actual research experience in Chisholm, Minnesota, of the ethereal ballplayer turned small-town doctor.

Archibald "Moonlight/Doc" Graham died at 85 in 1965 and is buried in Rochester, Minnesota. Chisholm and nearby Hibbing (birthplace of Bob Dylan) celebrate Doc "Moonlight" Graham Days every August. The event raises money to further the scholarship fund for underprivileged students that Graham set up with his estate upon his death. Even in death, Doc is doing the right thing.

For More Information: www.chisholmchamber.com

Thunder Bay Border Cats*/Port Arthur Stadium

425 Winnipeg Ave., Thunder Bay, ON, P7B 6P7
www.bordercatsbaseball.com

Western Ontario is home to Thunder Bay and the Border Cats every summer. The classic ballpark accented in Canadian red is welcoming and comfortable. The capacity of the ballpark is 3,035 and tickets are usually readily available.

---

*Located in the province of Ontario and less than 30 miles from the Minnesota border.

THE AMERICAN ASSOCIATION OF INDEPENDENT PROFESSIONAL BASEBALL

The American Association of Independent Professional Baseball (AAIPB) was founded in 2005 after the Central League collapsed and greater definition came to the independent baseball landscape in North America. The geography of the AAIPB stretches down a central swath of North America from Winnipeg, Saskatchewan, to Amarillo, Texas. Below are teams playing in the American Association of Independent Professional Baseball in Minnesota:

St. Paul Saints/Midway Stadium*

1771 Energy Park Dr., St. Paul, MN, 55108
(651) 644-6659 / www.saintsbaseball.com

Why the St. Paul Saints Matter...

Mike Veeck, co-owner of the very independent St. Paul Saints, may be one of the most important figures in the renaissance of minor league baseball over the past 25 years.

Less than 10 miles from Target Field and the Minnesota Twins of Major League Baseball, Mike Veeck is selling the St. Paul Saints as much today as the day he bought the team in 1993. The chorus of naysayers said they wouldn't survive because of the Twins being right down the street. Veeck responded by saying he had outdoor baseball and beer at a fraction of the cost. When the contrarians said he couldn't fill St. Paul's Midway Stadium, he put up promotions on a nightly basis that did just that.

"Never" has never been a word in Mike Veeck's vocabulary. Today, Veeck is chairman of a consortium that owns many minor league teams, including the Saint Paul Saints. Their business philosophy is simple: "fun is good." With the success of this new model in the early 1990s came a generation of more sophisticated ownership groups

---

*Ground broke August, 2013 for new stadium to open in 2015.

at the minor league level. Minor league baseball, once considered a costly but necessary anchor around the necks of the big-league clubs, is now considered big business.

What followed were new ballparks and major stadium renovations throughout minor league baseball. Minor league baseball owners owe a debt of gratitude to Mike Veeck for being a pioneer and taking chances two decades ago when most minor league organizations teams considered the smallest of crowds on a promotion night a success.

In 2015, the independent team that could will be moving into a new 7,500-seat stadium on the light rail line in St. Paul. No doubt, the St. Paul Saints are a must-see road trip stop in Minnesota.

CHAPTER 7

MISSOURI

· ·

Mark Twain, Old Muddy, and Killer BBQ

BUSCH STADIUM
Home of the St. Louis Cardinals

700 Clark Ave, St. Louis, MO, 63102
(314) 345-9600 / www.explorestlouis.com

The St. Louis Cardinals moved from old Busch Stadium to new Busch Stadium in 2006, promptly won the World Series in their inaugural year, and never looked back. The Cardinals organization started out things at the new Busch Stadium by creating history and reminding fans of their winning tradition.

The Cardinals have a tradition that competes with any in Major League Baseball and a fan base that measures out among the top five in baseball. The two things that made the St. Louis Cardinals popular were the fact they established the model for the current minor league development ladder and the invention of the radio. The Cardinals had "farm teams" all over the Midwest and throughout the mid-South well before formal leagues of affiliated teams were the norm. The Cardinals cornered the pick of the litter when the rest of baseball was depending on scattered scouts running into the next Honus Wagner. This helped develop a championship callous for the Cardinals as baseball transitioned into the modern era.

The growth of the team's following came with the invention of radio. KMOX in St. Louis is a 50,000-watt blowtorch of an AM radio station with a reach north into Canada, south into Mexico, and 750 miles east and west of St. Louis. Grandmothers and grandfathers, fathers and mothers of current Cardinals faithful were weaned on the radio calls of Harry Caray and Jack Buck for over a half a century. If you weren't watching the Cardinals at Sportsman's Park, you were listening to the Cardinals on the radio. If you lived in the Mississippi Valley, you may have grown up watching a Cardinals farm team then listening to KMOX from far-off St. Louis. For generations now, the St. Louis Cardinals have been a big part of people's lives wherever the Big Muddy flows through the middle of America.

SIDE TRIP: A ROAD TRIP WITH MARK TWAIN ON THE MIGHTY MISSISSIPPI

> "Baseball is the very symbol, the outward and visible expression of the drive and push and rush and struggle of the raging, tearing, booming nineteenth century." —*Mark Twain*

The Mississippi River is both friend and foe to folks who live along it. On one hand, it gives. Commerce and farming thrive in this fertile delta when it is calm. Jobs are safe and families are fed when the Mississippi River is their friend. On the other hand, it takes. Floods destroy farmland and wreak havoc on cities and towns along its mighty shores. The Mississippi River is a true wonder to ponder and enjoy up close.

Samuel Clemens (aka. Mark Twain) wrote a number of his finest works with the Mississippi River as a backdrop. America got to know about life on the Big Muddy through *The Adventures of Tom Sawyer* (1876) and *The Adventures of Huckleberry Finn* (1885). I recommend seeing the Mississippi River and a lot of great ballparks of the Midwest along the way by car on a five-day road trip.

Day 1: A great place to start is St. Louis. All major airlines fly there and rental cars are abundant. You can hit Busch Stadium that day for a game or a tour (if the Cardinals are on the road).

Day 2: Drive to Peoria, Illinois, on Interstate 55/155 and see Dozer Park and its palm trees. Peoria is home to the Cardinals' Midwest League affiliate (the Chiefs) and considered a key commercial hub for Midwestern farming.

Day 3: Drive to Galesburg, Illinois, to see the last standing site of a Lincoln-Douglas debate at Knox College. Then take a short drive to Davenport to see beautiful Modern Woodmen Park and the Quad Cities Bandits.

Day 4: Take a short trip from Davenport to Clinton, Iowa, to see Ashford University Field, home of the Midwest League's Lumber Kings. In the afternoon, start working south on the river on Iowa's State Roads 67 and 61 to see a game that evening at comfortable Community Field in Burlington, Iowa.

Day 5: Follow that river on S.R. 67 out of Iowa and hit Missouri again. Drive on Missouri State Roads 24 and 36 to visit Mark Twain's Boyhood Home in Hannibal in the morning. Have lunch and head south on State Road 61 and Interstate 70 East back to St. Louis to catch a Cardinals game or decompress before flying home.

The Cardinals fifth stadium makes a statement. The previous Busch Stadium was often compared to a spaceship. The spate of neo-modern stadiums in the late 1960s and 1970s that popped up in places like Cincinnati, Pittsburgh, and St. Louis looked to some more like a portal to a distant universe than a ballpark. These stadiums were massive structures made of concrete, steel, and paint and meant for multiple sports. They were ugly, plain and simple.

The ownership of the St. Louis Cardinals had no intention of replicating even the smartest features of old Busch Stadium in new Busch Stadium. The new Busch Stadium, designed by Populous, is easy to maneuver, stylish to the core, and one of the best ballparks in baseball. Cardinals fans have a new Mecca in new Busch Stadium and plan on coming back as much as they can once they get there.

The entire stadium project is a development plan that was done in phases. First, give the fans a great stadium representative of their winning tradition. The ballpark was opened in 2006. Second, iron out the deficiencies over the next few years to make it as perfect a ballpark as possible. Third, build a community around the ballpark that demands the attention of the fans not only before and after the game, but on a 365-day-a-year basis.

The most recent upgrade beyond Busch Stadium is the Ballpark Village. This area north of the ballpark is a mixed-use development with restaurants, retail shops, and residential units. The Cardinals Hall of Fame is located within this transitional area, as well as the Cardinals Nation restaurant and a Budweiser Brew House (over 100 taps with no repeating brands). For the ultimate diehard Cardinals fan with an addiction to his or her team and the means to live here, Ballpark Village is heaven. The Ballpark Village area will be completed in full before the start of the 2014 season.

The large fan base and the beautiful new ballpark make Busch Stadium a tough ticket. Be sure to plan ahead and see when tickets go on sale online for the Cardinals. In bad years, the Cardinals can depend on 3 million ticket buyers. Considering there are 46,000 seats and only 81 games a year, the closer you get to game time, the tougher it gets to find tickets. Plan ahead.

The Cardinals ownership is building a community to fit the lifestyle that is being a Cardinals fan. For years, Cardinal fans flocked to Wrigleyville and Wrigley Field to thump the Cubs then come home to a spaceship-like stadium that oozed zero charisma and was surrounded by a massive parking lot. That is no longer the case with new Busch Stadium and the adjoining Ballpark Village. The entire game day is vibrant, a 12-hour experience that is fun for baseball fans of all ages.

Fans will be happy to know that Busch Stadium allows food and drink (of the soft variety) into the ballpark. Coolers must be 16x16x8 and fit under your seat. You don't have to bring a cooler into the game, but you may want to consider filling a cooler with bottled water and ice to keep in the car. St. Louis is hot and muggy a lot of the summer and water is a necessity. A small bag cooler for the walk to the ballpark would be perfect. Remember to buy one with ample pockets for your peanuts or sunflower seeds.

You are not going to get many price breaks when it comes to the concession menu at Busch Stadium. Prices rival those at ballparks in much bigger cities. Even the "deal" price for the bottomless barrel of popcorn is $14.00. How much popcorn can one eat? Even the single-serve portion of $5.00 seems pricy for popcorn.

The joke at old Busch Stadium is that you could get both types of beer: Budweiser and Bud Light. This Anheuser-Busch-loyal city hasn't changed much, but it has benefited from the multiple options that came to town with the Anheuser-Busch/InBev deal. You can get just about every American craft beer InBev distributes at the new Busch Stadium. This is a big victory for beer fans.

The food menu at Busch Stadium is different, to say the least. The concessionaires and the Cardinal organization pushes people on buying sausages or sandwiches as a "deluxe basket" (with chips). You have no options beyond the chips and the prices range from $11.00 to $14.00 for these baskets. They are selling you a deal that is really not a deal. If you have to eat at the ballpark, opt for the much cheaper pretzel dog at $6.00. Honestly, St. Louis has much better food outside of the ballpark. While Busch Stadium is aesthetically beautiful, the ballpark needs to pick up their game. They have a Hardee's fast food restaurant in Busch Stadium but no place to buy the St. Louis delicacy toasted ravioli? That needs to be fixed.

One thing to their culinary credit is Busch Stadium's hot dog station sponsored by the Food Network on the third-base concourse. You can load up on certain types of encased meats purchased at this particular stand. The new addition of Kahn's Kosher Deli gives me hope. Another plus is the Farmer's Market by section 136 (by the Hardee's) if you are looking to get away from the typical ballpark fare.

Don't get me wrong: there are a lot of food options at Busch Stadium. There are lots of quality food options at Busch Stadium. What doesn't add up is the value of the food options at Busch Stadium. The prices do not fit the items offered. A stadium that draws 3 million people a year at an average of $112.00 a ticket should not be selling their cheapest hot dogs for $6.00. Drop the concession prices 30 percent across the board at Busch Stadium and you'll draw 3 million when the Cardinals have that off year as they do every once in a while.

But Cardinals fans are loyal and keep coming back to Ballpark Village. The fans of the Cardinals are among the most knowledgeable in the game. You will also get a good dose of tradition and reverence for the Cardinals greats throughout their almost 125-year existence. Statues of Dizzy Dean, "Cool Papa" Bell, Stan "The Man" Musial, Enos Slaughter, Rogers Hornsby, George Sisler, Jack Buck, and Ozzie Smith are dotted throughout the concourse adjacent to Gate 3.

You will have a better than average chance to meet Fredbird, the Cardinals mascot. Fredbird is a "newer" Cardinals tradition, having come along in 1979. Nonetheless, Fredbird is beloved by the Cardinals fans and Fredbird gets around the place. He has the energy of an actual cardinal—Fredbird stops only for kids and playful adults acting like kids. Fredbird often nests at the family friendly U.S. Cellular Family Pavilion.

Fredbird will jump on you if you are not wearing red. You will get stares if you are not wearing red from Cardinals fans, too. Everyone wears red at Busch Stadium. Supporters of opposing teams wearing the kit and color of their team get playfully heckled by Cardinals fans. Rest easy, know you are outnumbered, and laugh it off. The Cardinals fans are intelligent baseball fans and don't get into the mob mentality— despite everyone wearing cardinal red.

Because of that large, rabid fan base, the Cardinals offer four tours a day of Busch Stadium during the season and two tours a day during the off-season. There are no tours on holidays. The Busch Stadium tour is considered among the best in baseball and gives fans a thorough behind-the-scenes look at a great new ballpark.

Busch Stadium is a thing of beauty, a ballpark that sticks out from the crowd of recent retro-ballparks and welcomes fans wearing any color. Fans can reach St. Louis by plane easily since every major airline services the city directly. St. Louis is effectively Amtrak's hub terminus going back as long as the Cardinals have been around. St. Louis is at a point on the map where almost 50 percent of the United States can reach the city within an eight-hour drive. There, you have no excuses: get to beautiful Busch Stadium.

 Ballpark Facts, Figures, & Tips

The St. Louis baseball organization has not always been nicknamed the Cardinals. In their first 18 years after being founded in 1882, they were nicknamed the Browns, the Brown Stockings, and the Perfectos before being named the Cardinals…The first pitch at the new Busch Stadium is proof you should never have active players throw out a first pitch. Chris Carpenter and Albert Pujols were given the honor to do so on April 10, 2006. Carpenter's career was ended within a few years of that pitch and "Cardinal Forever" Albert Pujols left to play for the Los Angeles Angels in 2012…Over half a million hot dogs are eaten at Busch Stadium each season…The Cardinals organization is in annual contention for Major League

Baseball's organization of the year by *Baseball America* magazine…The Cardinals were purchased from the Busch family in 1996, however the presence of the former brewing family's name is all over the ballpark and they are a vital contributor to many St. Louis charities…The Cardinals boast 40 National Baseball Hall of Famers…The new Busch Stadium cost just over $410 million and the Cardinals financed over 90 percent of the project…The Cardinals' television partner, FOX Sports Midwest, draws the second largest audience on average among major league teams…The Cardinals' radio network flagship KMOX has almost 120 affiliates up and down the central swath of America and can reach 21 million fans…St. Louis was a two-team town for over 50 years until the crosstown Browns moved to Baltimore and became the Orioles in 1954…The Cardinals organization recycling and environmental efficiency programs are considered among the most effective in the MLB…The Cardinals Hall of Fame Museum is considered among one of the best curated baseball museums because of the extensive collection of memorabilia warehoused by the team since 1882.

 Best Tips for Seating

To sun or not to sun, that is the question at Busch Stadium. St. Louis loves their day games and in the summer that can get hot and muggy in this most famous of river towns. Plot your ticket purchase to either get the most shade as you can or best access to the covered concourse if you go to a day game in the summer. The heat and humidity can be taxing. This is a sunny stadium, even well into a mid-summer's night game, so be prepared to fight it.

Despite the normally high ticket prices and liberal use of the dynamic ticket pricing by the Cardinals organization, you can find a deal in the upper deck here and there. There are certain games of the year that certain upper-level seats can be found for as low as $5.00. Discount pricing does exist and you can look to the team website for credit card companies and organizations who offer discounts. AAA has certain deals for as much as half off tickets to the savvy baseball road trip planner. Check out the link on the Cardinals team website to the AAA page to grab great deals.

For the best deals combined with the best shade, look for the 300 level seats referred to as infield pavilion level seats. You can sit in comfort with a great view for $30.00 to $35.00 a ticket.

The brave of heart can have a great game experience in the outfield bleachers at Busch Stadium. Remember to bring your sun block and keep hydrated: the sun is tough out there.

Also, new Busch Stadium gets high marks for the increase in restrooms and concession stands compared to old Busch Stadium. Any ticketed customer will feel comfortable in their seat. Roaming around is a pregame luxury, also. The stadium was not designed with a 180 degree view from most of the concession/restroom areas of the concourse (a rarity for rock star stadium architect HOK/Populous).

 Driving Directions/Transportation

North, south, east, or west, a lot of major highways lead to St. Louis. From the north and south you have I-55. From the east, you have I-70 and I-64. From the west, you have I-44, I-64, and I-70. As mentioned before, St. Louis is accessible to a good chunk of people who live within the continental United States.

No matter where you are coming from, you will have to plan on hitting I-64 on your final leg to Busch Stadium. For those traveling from the north, south, and east of St. Louis, once you hit I-64 West, you will drive to Exit 40A that leads you to Stadium/Tucker Boulevard. You will then take right at Clark Street and the ballpark is within a block on the right.

For those traveling from the west of St. Louis, you will take Exit 40B that leads you to 6th Street. You will then exit left at Exit 39C which takes you to 11th Street. You will take a right at Clark Street and the ballpark is three blocks ahead on the right.

If you are staying in St. Louis, I recommend plotting out a hotel stay along their light rail system. MetroLink extends across the St. Louis metropolitan area and a round trip from your hotel will be less than $5.00.

 Parking

There are two main parking areas that bracket the Ballpark Village just north of Busch Stadium. In terms of parking, your options to park will range from expensive to more expensive ($20.00 to $30.00) for a mid-sized town like St. Louis. Lots are scattered south of the stadium and across I-64. You will pay less, but walk more.

 Airports

Lambert–St. Louis International Airport **(STL)** is an international airport serving the greater St. Louis region. The airport is 10 miles northwest of downtown St. Louis and is connected to the MetroLink system. St. Louis is a focus city for a number of major airlines.

 Car Rentals

St. Louis has more ground transportation options than most cities of its size. My first recommendation to people who will be hitting only the downtown St. Louis area is to use MetroLink, the public transportation option. However, if you are planning a regional road trip to ballparks in Illinois and Iowa, you will need a car. St. Louis has fewer rental company options than a Chicago or Minneapolis. However, these rental companies keep higher-than-normal inventories because

St. Louis has a higher-than-average corporate rental demand.

Alamo - (800) 462-5266
Avis - (800) 831-2847
Budget - (800) 527-0700
Enterprise - (800) 325-8007
Hertz - (800) 654-3131
National - (877) 222-9058
Thrifty - (800) 527-7075

 Dining/Bars/Nightlife

There are a lot of food and entertainment options in downtown St. Louis and near Busch Stadium. However, you will have not experienced St. Louis entirely until you have visited Italian Hill. The Hill, as it is known to locals, is south of I-44 between Hampton Avenue and the King's Highway. The Hill is home to over 30 Italian restaurants and 20 small shops selling diverse products. You won't have to go far from Busch Stadium to get to the Hill. It's a 10-minute trip from Ballpark Village.

No matter your tastes, St. Louis has ample options. Below is a list of places for breakfast, lunch, dinner, or a drink you may enjoy:

Adriana's—5101 Shaw Ave., St. Louis, MO, 63110
Charlie Gitto's—5226 Shaw Ave., St. Louis, MO, 63110
Lombardo's Trattoria—201 S. 20th St., St. Louis, MO, 63103
Mango—1101 Lucas Ave., St. Louis, MO, 63101
Pi Pizzeria—610 Washington Ave., St. Louis, MO, 63101
Sauce on the Side—903 Pine St., St. Louis, MO, 63101
Steve's Hot Dogs on the Hill—2131 Marconi Ave., St. Louis, MO, 63110
Ted Drewes Frozen Custard—6726 Chippewa St., St. Louis, MO, 63109
Tony's—410 Market St., St. Louis, MO, 63102
Zia's—5256 Wilson Ave., St. Louis, MO, 63110

Hotels/Accommodations

Courtyard by Marriott—2340 Market Street at Jefferson, St. Louis, MO, 63103, (866) 925-4218

Crowne Plaza—200 N. 4th Street, St. Louis, MO, 63102, (866) 767-0278

Doubletree Inn—1820 Market Street, St. Louis, MO, 63103, (866) 539-5067

Drury Inn—711 N. Broadway, St. Louis, MO, 63102, (866) 538-6252

Hampton Inn—333 Washington Ave., St. Louis, MO, 63102, (866) 538-1314

Hilton at the Ballpark—1 S. Broadway, St. Louis, MO, 63102, (866) 678-6350

Parkway Hotel—4550 Forest Park Ave., St. Louis, MO, 63108, (866) 538-0294

Renaissance—800 Washington Ave., St. Louis, MO, 63101, (866) 925-8676

Residence Inn—525 S. Jefferson Ave., St. Louis, MO, 63103, (866) 925-8709

The Westin—811 Spruce St., St. Louis, MO, 63102, (866) 573-4235

Ballpark/Neighborhood Security

St. Louis has a safer than average downtown area for a major U.S. city. This is a tourist area, so the St. Louis Police Department is going to patrol on a regular basis. On non-game nights, the city of St. Louis has a reputation where they roll up the sidewalks after people have left work and gone home to the suburbs. The Ballpark Village is providing a bridge to the downtown restaurant district and I can see a day where St. Louis has a vibrant downtown real estate market. Locals are approachable and more than willing to help tourists in St. Louis.

KAUFFMAN STADIUM
Home of the Kansas City Royals

1 Royal Way, Kansas City, MO, 64129
(800) 6-ROYALS / www.visitkc.com

The renovation of Kauffman Stadium in Kansas City between 2007 and 2009 took the relatively new (1973) ballpark out of the mid-20th century. The $256 million facelift was desperately needed and fans who attend ballgames there knew the update was overdue.

In 2006, I attended the opening home series at Kauffman Stadium with my wife and friends. We got to our section and met an usher who was roping off the section with the same yellow tape you see at murder scenes. A pipe above our ticketed section had burst. The Royals management handled the situation professionally by upgrading our seats for the game and giving us ticket vouchers for any home game for the rest of the year. Not being from Kansas City, we gave our vouchers to a young soldier we met who was serving at a nearby Army base. Throw in the fact the temperature was 22 degrees, and we still had a blast.

Kauffman Stadium is one-half of the Truman Sports Complex. The other half is Arrowhead Stadium, home of the Kansas City Chiefs. The parking lot itself is a spectacle to behold. The thing is a massive slab of asphalt that seems like one of the hottest places on the planet in the summer. Trees and shade are as rare as hen's teeth on this wide-open space of a complex. The bigness of the Truman Sports Complex will truly amaze you.

The updates to the ballpark itself included a massive video board and scoreboard, new seats, new sections, new outfield concourses, and improvements to the famous fountains beyond the outfield wall. Upon inquiry, I confirmed that plumbing updates were also done and better pipes were used in the renovation.

Another thing that has improved at Kauffman Stadium is the food.

What was once bland, basic ballpark fare is now among the most unique menus of any Major League Baseball park. Not many ballparks gamble with making barbeque, but you can land a rack of ribs, Kansas City brisket, pulled pork, and "burnt ends" (don't ask, just eat them; they're delicious) at the Kansas City All-Star Barbeque.

Yes, you can get that helmet full of nachos topped with a bunch of brisket. The Brisket-achos are a Kauffman Stadium favorite for fans who are into challenging their friends to a food contest.

The Kansas City Cantina taco truck on the new right-field complex offers fans Mexican options. The Urban Wok on the second level gives fans an Asian alternative to the smoked meat that dominates the ballpark. The burger, sausage, and hot dog options have been stepped up big time at Kauffman Stadium from just a decade ago. Fans can get foot-long brats and specialty burgers at the Diamond Grill on the home-plate concourse. In the late 1990s, barbequed ham was considered an exotic option at Kauffman Stadium. Things have changed for the better when it comes to food here.

Prices are reasonable at Kauffman Stadium, too. Being in the bread basket of America has its benefits and an ample supply leads to good prices for consumers. Beer and mixed drinks are still sold at a rate more suitable for Chicago or New York. However, prices across the board are lower than your average ballpark in the major leagues at Kauffman Stadium.

You do not have an exclusive situation when it comes to beer at Kauffman Stadium (meaning one dominant macro-brewer controlling all taps). Budweiser and MillerCoors products are sold and a ton of different microbrews are offered around the ballpark. Kansas City is a competitive beer market with an appreciation for micro- and nano-breweries. The fan wins on this front.

When you roam Kauffman Stadium, you will not suffer from a lack of entertainment. On the left-field concourse area, you can find the Royals Hall of Fame. A uniform-clad tour guide tells any interested party about the history of the ballclub and baseball in Kansas City. You get to see memorabilia from players who came through Kansas City on their way to baseball fame. You have players from the Kansas City Royals, Kansas City Monarchs (Negro Leagues), Kansas City A's, and the Kansas City Blues (Yankees powerhouse minor league team until 1954) in the Hall of Fame. You can learn about the ballparks for each program in the Hall of Fame and even plot a plan to visit the sites where they once stood.

The kids will not be bored at the K (what locals call Kauffman Stadium). The Kid Zone stretches across the left- and center-field concourses and features what seems to be every option in the world to keep a kid busy. Wiffle ball, a carousel, and a jungle gym will help tire out even the most energetic child. In a fit of brilliance, the Royals set up a kid-friendly concession stand and picnic area in this area. Parents will have all bases covered when they get to Kauffman Stadium.

But, the game is the primary reason you are at the ballpark, correct? Kauffman Stadium went to great lengths to ensure that your attention will be on the ballgame and that distractions on the concourse are confined to the concourse. This is a serious baseball town. Fans will engage you with conversations with high baseball intelligence. A fan will not get stares for taking score in Kansas City. Kansas City offers up some of the best atmosphere in baseball for fans of any type.

Truman Sports Complex is away from the downtown Kansas City area, so you will feel tucked away from the urban setting. This is not Wrigley Field or Fenway Park. You are in the middle of a massive parking lot in Middle America. There are a few hotels at the Truman Sports Complex interchange, but you will be limited for entertainment or dining options unless you get in your car and go downtown or to Country Club Plaza. Staying downtown is the better bet for fans. No matter what, you will need a car (Kansas City is not a public transportation city). However, driving around Kansas City isn't bad when you can hit great barbeque joints, the Negro League Hall of Fame, and classic architecture. You would be making a big mistake not taking in the food, fun, and atmosphere that make Kansas City a great city.

Kansas City and Kauffman Stadium is a great place for baseball fans to enjoy over a long weekend. The history, the fans, and the brand new ballpark make Kauffman Stadium a must-see destination these days for baseball travelers.

Ballpark Facts, Figures, & Tips

The K was renamed Kauffman Stadium after former Royals owner Ewing Kauffman in 1993. Previous to that, it was known as Royals Stadium…The entire Truman Sports Complex was built for $70 million. The recent renovation of Kauffman

Stadium alone cost $256 million…The renovation of Kauffman Stadium was designed by HOK Sport/Populous…In the fourth inning, people dressed in hot dog suits race for prizes and it will make you laugh…Royals Stadium was opened on April 10, 1973, with the Royals trouncing the Texas Rangers 12–1…The stadium has among the fewest suites in Major League Baseball with 35…Royals Stadium was the first stadium in baseball with artificial turf…The CrownVision scoreboard is second in size only to the LED scoreboard at Cowboys Stadium…The ballpark is owned by Jackson County and the Royals will be tenants until at least 2031.

Best Tips for Seating

With the renovation of Kauffman Stadium by HOK/Populous, what was a ballpark with very few flaws when it came to a view became a better place to watch a ballgame. Even though the view is great in the upper deck, you will be exposed to the sunlight. The ticket prices upstairs make it tempting to put up with the unforgiving sun. The party decks in the outfield have a growing reputation for a good view and a great time. The average crowds at Kansas City are around 57 percent capacity. So, good seats and deals can be found on most nights. Seats in the right- and left-field corners should be avoided because of their angle.

Driving Directions/Transportation

If you are coming from the east, head into Kansas City on I-70 until you hit Exit 9 (Blue Ridge Cutoff/Truman Sports Complex). You will be routed into the ballpark complex from this point.

If you are coming from the west, head into Kansas City on I-70 until you hit Exit 7B (Manchester Trafficway). You will turn left at this point and go to Gate 5 or take Exit 9 (Blue Ridge Cutoff/Truman Sports Complex). You will be routed into the ballpark complex from this point.

If you are coming from the south, head into Kansas City on I-435. Take Exit 63C (Raytown Road/Stadium Drive/Sports Complex). The ballpark complex is within eyeshot at this point.

If you are coming from the north, head into Kansas City on I-435. Take Exit 63B (I-70 East/Sports Complex exit) or Exit 63A (I-70 West) then take Exit 7B (Manchester Trafficway). You will then turn left and proceed to Gate 5.

There are no practical public transportation options connecting downtown Kansas City and Kauffman Stadium. The city has been developing a light rail system since 2007, but movement and money has been glacial in speed. A $20 million federal grant was given to Kansas City in September 2013, which will take care of the first phase (or 20 percent) of construction. That focus is the downtown route. The Truman Sports Complex is away from the downtown area and likely within the last phases of the project. The priority for cities is to connect airports with downtown areas with light rail. Kansas City International is on the opposite side of town from the Truman Sports Complex. In other words, it will be a long time before light rail gets to Kauffman Stadium.

Parking

The Truman Sports Complex has the biggest parking lot I have ever seen for a ballpark since I laid eyes on the Astrodome parking lot in Houston. The parking lot has ample spots for fans with vehicles of all sizes. Small cars can park for $10.00. Large trucks and recreational vehicles will cost you $15.00 to $20.00 to park. If you can't find a parking spot at the K, then the Royals have sold too many tickets for the game.

Airport

Kansas City International Airport (KCI) is a comfortable and functional airport serviced by all major airlines. The major complaints about the terminals center on the length of the terminals. A good walk never hurt anyone. There are complaints about the time it takes to process through TSA. There is no public transportation connected to Kansas City International Airport. Other than those factors, KCI is well-regarded by travelers and its mid-century design is pretty cool.

 ## Car Rentals

Once again, you will need a car in Kansas City. The light rail connection to the airport may happen in more than a decade, at best. Inventory at KCI can get tight, so plan well. Below is a list of car rental companies that operate out of Kansas City International Airport:

ACE - (816) 464-2100
Alamo - (816) 464-5151
Avis - (816) 243-5760
Budget - (816) 243-5757
Dollar - (800) 800-4000
Enterprise - (816) 464-2500
Fox - (816) 464-2100
Hertz - (816) 243-5765
National - (816) 243-5770
Payless - (816) 464-2100
Thrifty - (816) 464-5600

 ## Dining/Bars/Nightlife

Anytime you ask four people from Kansas City about the best food in Kansas City, you will get 12 opinions. Rest assured all of them are correct. No matter what, you will have to have steak and barbeque at least once on your visit to Kansas City.

Steak lovers can get an incredible Kansas City strip at the **Golden Ox Restaurant** (1600 Genessee St. #100, Kansas City). The Golden Ox was founded in 1949 and is a perfect old-school chop house. For barbeque, you have a million options. Two great places for Kansas City–style barbeque on the Kansas side of the border are **Oklahoma Joe's** (3002 W. 47th St., Kansas City) and **LC's BBQ** (5800 Blue Pkwy., Kansas City) on the Missouri side of the border. LC's BBQ is just to the south of the Truman Sports Complex off of I-435.

Some other options in the Kansas City restaurant and bar market are listed below. My best advice is to make sure you have a salad for one meal a day because the steak and barbeque options will test your discipline:

Arthur Bryant's BBQ—1727 Brooklyn Ave., Kansas City, MO, 64127

B.B.'s Lawnside BBQ—1205 E. 85th St., Kansas City, MO, 64131

The Brick—1727 McGee St., Kansas City, MO, 64108

Danny Edwards Famous KC BBQ—2900 Southwest Blvd., Kansas City, MO, 64108

Green Room Burgers & Beer—4010 Pennsylvania Ave., Kansas City, MO, 64111

Grinders Pizza—417 E. 18th St., Kansas City, MO, 64108

Johnny Jo's Pizzeria—1209 W. 47th St., Kansas City, MO, 64112

Happy Gillis Hangout & Café—549 Gillis St., Kansas City, MO, 64106

McCoy's Public House—4057 Pennsylvania Ave., Kansas City, MO, 64111

Potpie—904 Westport Rd., Kansas City, MO, 64111

Hotels/Accommodations

Kansas City's Kauffman Stadium is southeast of the downtown area and has a few hotels around it. Unfortunately, the dining options are limited. The hotels near the ballpark are listed. However, most of the hotels listed are in downtown Kansas

City and an area called Country Club Plaza. Country Club Plaza has hundreds of shopping and dining options for visitors to consider.

Best Western Plus—4309 Main St., Kansas City, MO, 64111, (866) 925-8676
Courtyard by Marriott—4600 J.C. Nichols Pkwy., Kansas City, MO, 64112, (866) 925-4159
Drury Inn—3830 Blue Ridge Cut Off, Kansas City, MO, 64133, (866) 573-4235
Hampton Inn—4600 Summit Kansas City, MO, 64112, (866) 538-9298
Holiday Inn—1 E. 45th St., Kansas City, MO, 64111, (866) 573-4235
Holiday Inn CoCo Key—9103 E. 39th St., Kansas City, MO, 64133, (866) 573-4235
Holiday Inn Express—8551 E. Blue Pkwy., Kansas City, MO, 64133, (866) 925-4159
The Intercontinental—401 Ward Pkwy., Kansas City, MO, 64112, (866) 538-6252
Marriott—4445 Main St., Kansas City, MO, 64111, (866) 678-6350
Sheraton—770 W. 47th St., Kansas City, MO, 64112, (866) 539-5067

Ballpark/Neighborhood Security

Kauffman Stadium is within the wide-open Truman Sports Complex and not confined to a neighborhood like many ballparks in Major League Baseball. The stadium is among the safest in baseball. Incidents do occur in the parking lot, but those usually have to do with revelers and are very rare. You will have to consider where you are when you go back to your hotel district. Kansas City has the average random crime problem of any major city. Police patrols are extensive in the Country Club Plaza area due to the high concentration of tourists and visitors to the area.

THE FRONTIER LEAGUE

The Frontier League is a non-affiliated baseball league for college players. The teams are located in Illinois, Kentucky, Missouri, Ohio, and Pennsylvania. The Frontier League even has a traveling team (The Frontier Greys). Most players are "adopted" by local residents and live in spare rooms provided by their adopting family for the summer. Companies who support the teams often provide part-time jobs for players. Many Baseball America top 500 prospects play in the Frontier League. With some research, you can find a player or two of interest and check them out with a short side trip as part of your planned baseball road trip. Below is a list of Frontier League teams located in the state of Missouri:

River City Rascals/T.R. Hughes Ballpark

· ·

900 T.R. Hughes Blvd., O'Fallon, MO, 63366
(636) 240-2287 / www.rivercityrascals.com

The River City Rascals are lucky to play in this beautiful 3,687-seat ballpark. The fans of O'Fallon are fun and supportive of the Rascals.

For a Frontier League ballpark, this is among the tops for entertainment and value. O'Fallon is an hour west of St. Louis and three hours west of Kansas City and makes a perfect place off of I-70 to break up a drive.

THE AMERICAN ASSOCIATION OF INDEPENDENT PROFESSIONAL BASEBALL

The American Association of Independent Professional Baseball (AAIPB) was founded in 2005 after the Central League collapsed and greater definition came to the independent baseball landscape in North America. The geography of the AAIPB stretches down a central swath of North America from Winnipeg, Saskatchewan, to

SIDE TRIP: BREWERY TOURS BIG & SMALL IN MISSOURI

Interstate 70 across Missouri offers baseball and beer fans the ability to visit three great ballparks with towns that boast three great breweries.

In Kansas City, Boulevard Brewing Co. (2501 Southwest Blvd., Kansas City, MO, 64108) offers 15 year-round and seasonal beers. Reservations are required for a tour. A tour makes for a great way to fill a morning before an afternoon game at Kauffman Stadium. To reserve a tour, call (816) 474-7095. Their 80-Acre Hoppy Wheat Ale is exceptional.

Three hours east off of Interstate 70 is O'Fallon, T.R. Hughes Ballpark, and O'Fallon Brewery (26 West Industrial Dr., O'Fallon, MO, 63366). Reservations for a tour can be made at (636) 474-2337. O'Fallon has become popular with craft beer fans that enjoy fruitier bouquets and stronger flavors.

Of course, Anheuser-Busch is brewing in St. Louis (12th & Lynch St., St. Louis, MO, 63118). Call the brewery tour office for information at (314) 577-2626 or go online to check the hours for regular daily tours. Anheuser-Busch has different hours for the winter and summer and the tour groups are open and large.

Another option for a free brewery tour (only Friday through Sunday) is Schafly Bottleworks (7260 Southwest Ave., Maplewood, MO, 63143). This little brewery has a loyal following and produces four standard beers. Tours can be reserved at (314) 241-2337, ext. 285. Their Black IPA will tempt you to take some home with you.

Amarillo, Texas. Below is a team playing in the American Association of Independent Professional Baseball in Missouri and Kansas:

Kansas City T-Bones/Community America Ballpark

1800 Village West Pkwy., Kansas City, KS, 66111
(913) 328-2255 / www.tbonesbaseball.com

The 5,768-seat Community America Ballpark is a ballpark that serves as a centerpiece for the development of a commercial and retail business complex in the western suburbs of Kansas City. The "little green monster" makes the playing green stand out from the rest in the AAIPB. The ballpark is adjacent to the Kansas Motor Speedway complex.

CHAPTER 8

OHIO

. . . .

The Jake, the Mistake
by the Lake, and Driving
the Pete Rose Way

PROGRESSIVE FIELD
Home of the Cleveland Indians

• •

2401 Ontario St., Cleveland, OH, 44115
(216) 420-HITS / www.positivelycleveland.com

Clevelanders are a defiantly proud tribe. They see a beauty in their city that others may not readily understand on first glance. Cleveland has one foot on the East Coast and the other foot firmly in the Midwest. The buildings are mostly filled and classically built. The architecture reaches back to the days of John Rockefeller and Standard Oil's pre–New York days. The new architecture, though, looks forward while respecting that great past.

Progressive Field is a piece of Cleveland architecture that does just that. Many still call Progressive Field "The Jake" in a nod to the former name of the ballpark, Jacobs Field. Progressive Insurance purchased the naming rights to the stadium in 2008 for 16 years for $3.6 million a year. The front office can make as many deals as they like: most fans still call this place "The Jake."

Progressive Field was built in 1994, at which point the Indians moved from their old digs, Cleveland Municipal Stadium. Municipal Stadium was demolished in 1996 and with it many bad memories for Cleveland sports. The resident teams seemed vexed at the old ballpark. The same could not be said of the Indians and the Jake for the next half decade.

The Indians went on to win five straight American League Central Division championships. The team went on to represent the AL and lose the 1995 and 1997 World Series. However, Clevelanders came out in droves to see their new stadium and support their winning nine: between 1995 and 2001, Cleveland sold out Progressive Field (née Jacobs Field) 445 games in a row.

The Cleveland Indians were no longer a punch line. The curse that may or may not have come with their previous stadium known to many as "The Mistake by the Lake" may have been killed with the construction of this northeast Ohio gem.

As time passes and the winning seasons get fewer and far between, grabbing a ticket for a game at Progressive Field has become an easier task (average attendance in 2013 hovered at the 20,000 mark). The stadium's capacity is 43,545. You will be able to walk up to the ticket booth and most likely find tickets in a great section.

The best place for a group or set of families to rendezvous before heading into Progressive Field is Gate C. Like many other "retro" ballparks, Cleveland showed reverence to their baseball heroes and put a statue of Indians Hall of Fame pitcher Bob Feller at Gate C. For stadium statues, this statue of Rapid Robert is pretty good. The artist actually emulated the violent hurtling motion Feller famously employed in his pitching style. Once everyone gathers, Progressive Field is your oyster.

No matter where you sit in this comfortable stadium, you will find a pretty solid menu and beer selection at Progressive Field. The price point for standard ballpark fare is pegged below the average for major league ballparks. Fans can even get refills for their already large soda for $2.00. You are not going to get a big variety beyond hot dogs, burgers, and pizza at Progressive Field.

The concession stand at the ballpark that stands out with the most unique food offering is Cleats on the third-base concourse. Fans can get chicken wings in a variety of flavors at this stand. A Food Network concession stand sells macaroni and cheese and a few other tepid comfort-food choices.

Before the 2013 season started, the Indians organization lowered prices for concessions around the ballpark. When this is done by organizations, variety usually suffers on ballpark menus. However, Cleveland is now in the unique position to improve food choices and quality. The organization is moving forward on the field and as attendance grows, so will their options at the concession stand.

What Progressive Field isn't for foodies it is for beer connoisseurs. The stadium has held a longtime commitment to having beer options that range from the hipster chic to those that excite beer geeks. One particular stand ("Your Dad's Beers") sells canned, old-school beers like Blatz, Stroh's, and other nostalgic beers. Beer prices have been slashed for the more familiar labels under the Miller and Budweiser labels to $4.00 for a 12-ounce draft. Microbreweries like Great Lakes still have a good presence at the ballpark and offer a few handles at stands throughout the ballpark. The "Spirits of Ohio" stand on the home-plate concourse offers beers from quality Ohio microbreweries like Christian Moerlein, Mt. Carmel Brewing, and Thirsty Dog. This stand also offers great options for those looking for a quality mixed drink from outstanding Ohio distilleries.

Clevelanders and Indians fans are fans of the mustard named Bertman's Ballpark Mustard. The taste is somewhere between yellow mustard and a hearty horseradish mustard. The hue is more brown than yellow and the spice is tempered. Akin to Milwaukee's Stadium Sauce, it comes off as a blend rather than a unique flavor. Bertman's Ballpark Mustard is not offensive and should be tasted for the true Cleveland encased meat experience.

Progressive Field is remarkably well-kept for a stadium that is almost 20 years old. The cleanliness may be a "never again" response to the sooty and rough feel of old Municipal Stadium. Some joked that the demolition of the old ballpark was a step up when it came to cleanliness. Progressive Field is clean, almost to the point of anti-septic.

Antiseptic without coming off as one of the insincere throwback stadiums that popped up like mushrooms in the 1990s across the United States. The reverence for the past is appropriately displayed at the Indians Hall of Fame and Heritage Park off of the center-field concourse. This area is secluded and respectful of the past, almost like a grotto for prayers of the faithful. Jim Thome fans will be happy to know that a statue has been commissioned in his likeness for Heritage Park (to be completed before the 2014 season begins).

Where Municipal Stadium was not a place to take a family, Progressive Field is full of family fun. There is a large designated area for kids to enjoy interactive games and physical activity if things drag before or during the game. Parents should tend to the kids in shifts if they are baseball fans—there's no view of the game from the Indians Kid Clubhouse.

The crowds may have halved since the glory days of the 1990s, but the staff of Progressive Field is just as helpful and just as strict as they were when the place was newly minted and called "The Jake." Security and ushers will help you with anything; just make sure you are sitting in your ticketed seat. The fans are number one at Progressive Field, but make sure you are following the social contract and sticking to your section. It is guaranteed that you will be asked to see your ticket by an usher.

With the descent of fortunes for the Indians over the past decade, premium ticket pricing has been relaxed. You can find reasonably priced tickets for games once deemed premium. For the price, you don't get the chance to see the inside and outside of quality architecture like Progressive Field.

Ballpark Facts, Figures, & Tips

Former Cleveland Indians owner Richard Jacobs had an agreement for two years after selling the team in 1999 that the name of the ballpark could not be changed…Progressive Insurance is a born and bred Cleveland company with their corporate headquarters in the suburb of Mayfield Village… The $175 million ballpark was designed by HOK Sport (now Populous)…The stadium is owned by the county and operated by a designated economic development corporation…The inaugural opening day at "The Jake" saw the Cleveland Indians beat the Seattle Mariners 4–3 in extra innings… The Indians' record of 455 sellouts in a row at Jacobs Field between 1995 and 2001 was not broken until 2008 by the Boston Red Sox and Fenway Park…Progressive Field was getting awards for best ballpark in Major League Baseball (*Sports Illustrated*, 2008) almost 15 years into its existence.

Best Tips for Seating

Cleveland baseball fans are bullish on the outfield bleachers as a great deal with a great view. Bleachers run between $10.00 and $22.00 and are not a world away from the field.

Club seats above the first-base/right-field lower boxes are recommended if you want easy access to the amenities on the concourse. One comfort offered in this area is a wait staff who will take your order so you don't have to leave your seat and deal with lines. These tickets are pricey ($80.00 to $90.00) but the service and amenities can't be beat.

A good package for local fans to consider is membership in the Terrace Club. The terrace seats are more about comfort than it is about a view. Far down the line in the left-field corner, sitting in the club terrace is a casual way to get suite service. The packages for the Terrace Club vary in price and you will have to inquire with the Indians' ticket office on your options. This package may be perfect for a small business to buy to impress clients. A dress code exists, but it is still a more casual atmosphere for fans.

Driving Directions/Transportation

The area Progressive Field is in is called the Gateway Quarter. Three interstate highways pass by the immediate area and give easy access to the ballpark.

Fans can use I-90 from the east or west of the city and exit at 9th Street. You will be routed to parking almost immediately off of the exit.

From the south, fans can use I-77 and exit at either 9th Street or Ontario Street. Once again, you will have immediate parking options once off of the ramp.

If you are coming from the southwest, take I-71 to the Inner Belt merge. Take I-90 from there to 9th Street or Ontario Street. Signs will lead you to parking from the ramp at either street.

The Greater Cleveland Regional Transit Authority has three major lines that feed to the Tower City transit building. The walk from this rail hub is five to 10 minutes. The GCRTA is one of the best deals out there for the price you pay for an all-day pass: $5.00 for adults and $2.50 for kids.

Cleveland mass transit schedules and regional lines can be viewed at www.riderta.com.

The city of Cleveland runs circulator trolleys in the downtown area that pick up and drop off at Progressive Field. Be aware that the lines are named after letters in the alphabet and have specific routes, so changing trolleys will be necessary. You will want to plan your route at www.riderta.com/routes/trolley. The trolley system is an affordable way to get around the major sites of Cleveland. There are all-day passes available on the trolley fare box, the GCRTA vending machines, and retailers throughout the city.

Parking

Like any other stadium with ample parking, the closer you are to the ballpark, the more the parking will cost. In a remarkably efficient manner, Cuyahoga County and Cleveland have a color system for the price range of lots. Prices range from $5.00 to $20.00 for color-coded parking lots. There are specially priced garages that are actually connected to the ballpark that go for $12.00 and offer the best safety. This option is probably best. Parking around Progressive Field is like the three bears tasting porridge: the best option is likely the last one you find and then you will decide the price is just right. $12.00 is a pretty good price for parking in a major-city parking lot.

Airport

Cleveland Hopkins International Airport **(CLE)**

Car Rentals

Alamo - (800) 327-9633
Avis - (216) 265-3702
Budget - (800) 527-0700
Dollar - (800) 800-4000
Enterprise - (800) 736-8222
Hertz - (800) 654-3131
National - (800) 227-7367
Thrifty - (800) 847-4389

Dining/Bars/Nightlife

Cleveland is now a foodie's paradise because of Michael Symon. The James Beard Award–winning chef raised the bar for the whole Cleveland restaurant scene with **Lola** (2058 E. 4th St., Cleveland) in the Gateway District. The chic bistro drew attention toward the existing quality restaurants in Cleveland and drew new restaurants that have changed how the cuisinistas of America view Cleveland.

Just up the street from Lola is **Chinato** (2079 E. 4th St., Cleveland). Their menu of Italian rustic and upscale selections rarely disappoints. For a little more downscale and for your fix of sports, wings, and burgers in the Gateway District, hit the **Winking Lizard Tavern** (811 Huron Rd. E., Cleveland). For a great pizza experience in downtown Cleveland, try the pie at **Vincenza's Pizza & Pasta** (603 Prospect Ave. E., Cleveland).

For a beer or quality whiskey before or after the game in the Gateway District, you cannot go wrong with **Flannery's** (323 E. Prospect Ave., Cleveland). Cleveland has a sizeable Irish population and better-than-average Irish pubs like Flannery's dot the landscape.

A few other selections to consider in Cleveland's ethnically diverse neighborhoods (in parentheses) are listed below:

Nate's Deli & Restaurant (Ohio City)—1923 W. 25th St., Cleveland, OH, 44113

Solokowski's Polish Restaurant (Tremont)—1201 University Rd., Cleveland, OH, 44113

Slyman's Restaurant (Goodrich Kirtland)—3106 Saint Clair Ave N.E., Cleveland, OH 44114

Hotels/Accommodations

Aloft—1111 W. 10th Street Cleveland, OH, 44113, (866) 538-6252

Comfort Inn—1800 Euclid Ave., Cleveland, OH, 44115, (866) 925-4159

The Cleveland Hostel—2090 W. 25th St., Cleveland, OH, 44113, (216) 394-0616

Doubletree Suites—1111 Lakeside Ave. E. Cleveland, OH, 44114, (866) 573-4235

Hampton Inn—1460 E. 9th St. Cleveland, OH, 44114, (866) 678-6350

Hyatt Regency—420 Superior Ave. E. Cleveland, OH, 44114, (866) 925-1043

Marriott Downtown—127 Public Sq., Cleveland, OH, 44114, (866) 767-0278

Radisson—651 Huron Rd. E. Cleveland, OH, 44115, (866) 678-6350

Tudor Arms Hotel—10660 Carnegie Ave., Cleveland, OH, 44106, (866) 539-9234

Ballpark/Neighborhood Security

American cities tout the word "revitalization" when it comes to their downtown areas, but a lot of the time it is a coat of paint on a bunch of buildings around a mega-mall or new stadium. Cleveland is not that city and the Gateway District is a prime example of how a stadium district can drive regrowth in a diverse, urban economy.

The city of Cleveland has worked on a security plan in the Gateway District that keeps locals and tourists alike very safe. This is still an urban setting and crime does exist. However, you should feel very safe in Cleveland. Progressive Field is better than the vast majority of Major League Baseball stadiums when it comes to safety. You should have a good and safe visit to this lovely ballpark.

GREAT AMERICAN BALLPARK
Home of the Cincinnati Reds

· ·

100 Joe Nuxhall Way, Cincinnati, OH, 45202
(877) 647-REDS / www.cincinnatiusa.com

When you attend a game at Great American Ballpark in Cincinnati, you get the feeling the city was just trying to play catch-up with the rest of baseball when it came to getting a new ballpark. After 30-plus years at the droll Riverfront Stadium, the local planners were all for a modern/retro ballpark like Baltimore's Camden Yards or Progressive Field in Cleveland.

Unfortunately, Cincinnati built a ballpark that felt as if it was still under construction even though it was open for business. The grandstands and bleachers gave the impression to viewers on television that the ballpark was a slick jewel. However, when fans came into the ballpark and walked the concourse, they found empty gaps where concession stands or restrooms should have been. Over time, many of these gaps have been filled hastily by the city and county stadium authority.

So slow was the transition of Cincinnati's Great American Ballpark into maturity that Major League Baseball will not grant it an All-Star Game until 2015. Typically, a new ballpark gets this privilege within a few years of construction to aid in its development. Great American Ballpark opened in 2003.

Despite the slow start, the Great American Ballpark has come into its own and more. It is slowly becoming a great place to experience a baseball game.

The Reds organization was founded in 1869 and Cincinnati is a city steeped in baseball history. The ballpark took advantage of the lush background of the Kentucky side of the Ohio River. The famous Cincinnati hillside skyline is behind the ballpark and still a strong influence that shadows the ballpark.

Baseball history matters to Cincinnati and this ballpark pays homage to that storied past. You will enter the ballpark in a plaza named Crosley Terrace. Crosley Field was the home of the Reds for 58 years until Riverfront Stadium came along in 1971. Crosley Terrace has an innovative set of statuary featuring Reds greats Ernie Lombardi catching, Joe Nuxhall pitching, Ted Kluszewski on deck, and Frank Robinson at bat. The street that leads to this plaza is technically called Joe Nuxhall Way. You can't but smile absorbing this history and enjoying this walk.

Before you head in, get a long look at Cincinnati's skyline and try to get over to the Roebling Suspension Bridge. Cincinnati has beautiful architecture in their buildings and a number of great bridges. Roebling was the designer of the Brooklyn Bridge, too. Views of the skyline and river can be taken in from the concourse inside the ballpark, as well.

Once inside the ballpark, the Reds invite you to their Hall Of Fame. Don't go. The Reds organization has the largest hall of fame in baseball for a reason: it seems as if they put everybody who played more than 10 games as a Red in the Hall of Fame. Plus, the price is frankly prohibitive ($10.00) considering you are still holding a very expensive ticket in your hand.

Once again, the concourse is not going to thrill you from an aesthetics standpoint. I am sure they will have figured it out by the 2015 All-Star Game. You will make your way to what amounts to a comfortable seating area with room to spare for you and your legs. Some seats are more equal than others at Great American Ballpark: the closer to the outfield seats and upper decks you get, the tighter your seats.

Not all seats afford a good view of the game, the video board, and scoreboards. There are certain seats in left field that have a great view of the game, but no view of the scoreboard. If you have a seat where the game scoreboard can be seen, you will be entertained with a scoreboard that offers a lot of information.

You will notice immediately that the stadium is designed to look like a riverboat. The light standards have the look of smoke stacks on a riverboat. The trim is cut to look like that on the walkways of a riverboat. A deck has been built in center field called the Riverboat. You get everything riverboat at Great American Ballpark except the gambling.

Seating at any level of Great American Ballpark is a gamble, so investigate. Price does not necessarily equate to comfort at this stadium. Choose carefully.

What may sway your opinion immediately to the positive about Great American Ballpark is a visit to the concession stand. Cincinnati appreciates good food. The ballpark has foods ranging from basic ballpark food to well-known Cincinnati restaurants. The sausages are better than most in baseball because Cincinnati is a German town with a great history of producing great encased meats.

In Cincinnati, there are hot dogs (Kahn's) and metts. A mett is a beef hot dog with cheese built into the frankfurter. This is a Cincinnati thing because I grew up around a lot of people of German descent in the Midwest and a metwurst is something completely different from a cheese and encased meat product. But, as with anything sausage, you can always find enough sauerkraut and mustard to make it edible. Fans of Skyline Chili can grab their famous coney dog with onions and the pile of cheese so high that a Sherpa is required to scale it. Prices for their specialty dogs are very affordable compared to other ballparks.

You will see Mr. Red all over Great American Ballpark but his favorite place to hang out is Mr. Red's Smokehouse in the right-field corner. This is where the bulk of non-sausage specialty plates are found. For $20.00, you can get an excellent pulled pork sandwich, corn on the cob, and a domestic pulls. That's a lot of money, but for this combination at a ballpark, you are getting a deal.

Two other specialty plates served by Mr. Red are Kobe beef sliders and the State Fair–like turkey leg. Stick with the sliders if you don't want the shame of hoisting a greasy stick of bird for three innings. They also have a decent selection of beers at Mr. Red's Smokehouse.

Another Cincinnati favorite is served at Great American Ballpark: LaRosa's Pizza. LaRosa's cheese/sauce/crust combination complement each other very well. This longtime regional favorite would be a national chain but they are obsessed with quality at LaRosa's. Enjoy what this writer considers one of the five best pizzas you likely have heard of but never tasted. LaRosa's is wonderful.

Being in the bread basket of America and being that Cincinnati is a very family-friendly ballpark, it only makes sense that the Reds offer a Farmer's Market on each concourse of the stadium. Someone in the front office had their noggin working when they conceived the Great American Ballpark Farmer's Market. The fruits, vegetables, and medical supplies are common-sense items we just don't think about at a ballgame.

The cooling stations are also places to plot out before you take your seat. Cincinnati is a hot town and especially muggy in mid-summer. Take advantage of these zones before and after hitting the bathroom during the game. Speaking of the bathrooms, the stadium authority should make it a priority to improve lighting in bathroom areas before the 2015 All-Star Game.

If you have any difficulties, the staff at Great American Ballpark is exceptionally helpful. They are strict on ticketing the closer games get to sellouts. The best policy is to keep your seat and roam about the concourse on your level to see the sights.

No matter where you sit, no matter where you roam, no matter what you eat at Great American Ballpark, you will find a good time. The fans love their Reds baseball and the staff will make you feel welcome. A trip to the new and improved ballpark called Great American Ballpark is becoming a must-do for baseball travelers who love history, baseball, and a good time.

Ballpark Facts, Figures, & Tips

The stadium was opened in March 2003 at a cost of just over $290 million...The first game played on March 28, 2003, was a 10–1 exhibition game loss to the Pittsburgh Pirates...The HOK Sport–designed stadium took just under three years for the Hunt Construction Group to complete...The address of 100 Joe Nuxhall Way is actually a renamed extension of Cincinnati's Main Street...The sculptures in Crosley Terrace of Reds greats Lombardi, Nuxhall, Kluzsewski, and Robinson were all done by artist Thomas Tsuchiya...The Great American Insurance company owns the naming rights to the ballpark run by the Hamilton County Stadium Authority until 2033 at an annual cost of $2.5 million...This is the seventh home for the

Reds. Four of those ballparks were used from 1869 to 1911. The Reds have had three stadiums in the past century: Crosley Field, Riverfront Stadium, and Great American Ballpark…Reds attendance is usually based on how the Reds are doing and whether the stadium authority is keeping prices low. Tickets are available, but check ahead if the Reds are in a winning way.

Best Tips for Seating

The position of every seat in Great American Ballpark is biased toward the field. The good bulk of the ballpark seats, no matter their level, will make you happy according to the budget you bring to the ballpark. However, blind spots are aplenty in the left-field bleachers, so avoid them if you can. Also, upgrading your seat is tough but a lot easier on low-attendance days.

Driving Directions/Transportation

The two main highways that run through Cincinnati are I-71 and I-75. If you stay true to these highways and miss Great American Ballpark or Pete Rose Way that leads you to the ballpark, you are not in Cincinnati. Both of these major highways have ample signage that will lead you to the downtown/stadium district no matter where you are staying in the Cincinnati/Kentucky area.

Parking

Expensive parking for Reds games in the stadium zone or near downtown will run you an average of $15.00, which is very affordable, compared to the rest of baseball. The area around the stadium zone is built for parking and dependent on what series you are seeing or how well the Reds are doing, you will be able to find parking closer to your seats than you may expect.

Airport
Cincinnati-Northern Kentucky International Airport (CVG)

Car Rentals
Alamo - (800) 327-9633
Avis - (800) 331-1212
Budget - (800) 527-0700
Dollar - (800) 800-4000
Enterprise - (800) 325-8007
Hertz - (800) 654-3131
National - (800) 328-4567
Thrifty - (800) 367-2277

Dining/Bars/Nightlife
Cincinnati is a food town, but you will have to drive to find some of the best places. Jimmy G's (435 Elm St., Cincinnati) is a solid steakhouse within a walk from most downtown hotels. Cincinnati's most famous barbeque joint may be the **Montgomery Inn** (925 Riverside Dr., Cincinnati), but **Eli's BBQ** (3313 Riverside Dr., Cincinnati) is setting standards that may make it the best barbeque in Cincinnati.

I am a fan of Mount Adams because of its eclectic shops and excellent nightlife. **Crowley's** (958 Pavilion St., Cincinnati) on Mount Adams may be the least pretentious bar in Cincinnati. For the best view of the Cincinnati skyline at any time of the day, go to **City View Tavern** (403 Oregon St., Cincinnati) on Mount Adams. Their basic burger with chips and a beer hit the spot every time.

You also should make an effort to head up to the Camp Washington neighborhood to enjoy a nationally recognized treasure, **Camp Washington Chili** (3005 Colerain Ave., Cincinnati). Camp Washington Chili is constantly being recognized by magazines and food observers as an iconic restaurant that represents Cincinnati's culinary contribution to the United States: good Cincinnati-style chili.

Other restaurants to consider when in Cincinnati/northern Kentucky:

LaRosa's—1250 W. 8th St., Cincinnati, OH, 45203, (513) 347-1111 (Pizza)
Nicola's—1420 Sycamore St., Cincinnati, OH, 45202, (513) 721-6200 (Italian)
Ollie's Trolley—1607 Central Ave., Cincinnati, OH, 45214, (513) 381-6100
Paula's—41 E. 4th St., Cincinnati, OH, 45202, (513) 381-3354 (Burgers)
Skyline Chili—643 Vine St., Cincinnati, OH, 45202, (513) 241-2020 (Chili)
Walt's Hitching Post—3300 Madison Pike, Fort Wright, KY, 41011, (859) 360-2222 (BBQ/Ribs)

Hotels/Accommodations

The Cincinnatian—601 Vine St., Cincinnati, OH, 45202, (513) 381-3000
Four Points—150 W. 5th St., Cincinnati, OH, 45202, (513) 357-5800
The Garfield—2 Garfield Pl., Cincinnati, OH, 45202, (513) 421-3355
Hilton—35 W. Fifth St., Cincinnati, OH, 45202, (513) 421-9100
Hyatt Regency—151 W. 5th St., Cincinnati, OH, 45202, (513) 579-1234
Millennium Hotel—141 W. 6th St., Cincinnati, OH, 45202, (513) 352-2100
Quality Inn—800 W. 8th St., Cincinnati, OH, 45202, (513) 241-8660
Residence Inn—506 E. 4th St., Cincinnati, OH, 45202, (513) 651-1234

Symphony Hotel—210 W. 14th St. Cincinnati, OH, 45202, (513) 721-3353

The Westin—21 E. 5th St., Cincinnati, OH, 45202, (513) 621-7700

Ballpark/Neighborhood Security

Cincinnati is a safer-than-usual town with crime statistics comparable to other Midwestern American cities like Indianapolis or Cleveland. Cincinnati is a car city: you will need your car to get around unless you have the phone number of a quality cab company in your pocket.

Great American Ballpark is located in a stadium zone adjacent to a development zone that is mostly filled with restaurants and bars. You can walk Cincinnati, but walking across the bridge from Kentucky's hotels may be a risky proposition. If you have your coordinates down for your hotel and your mode of transportation lined up, you should be okay getting around safely in the Queen City.

HUNTINGTON PARK
HOME OF THE COLUMBUS CLIPPERS

AAA Affiliate of the Cleveland Indians/
International League

· ·

330 Huntington Park Lane, Columbus, OH, 43215
(614) 462-5250 / www.clippersbaseball.com

The people of Columbus, Ohio, have a top-of-the-line stadium in Huntington Park. Opened in 2009, the 12,150-seat stadium can give some major league parks a run for their money when it comes to design and amenities. The fans of Columbus also have a good view no matter where they sit.

Huntington Park is an economic development tool that goes beyond the turnstiles for Columbus. Many businesses are integrated into the stadium design. The downtown skyline stands beyond the outfield and into the distance saying Columbus is a state capital, major university town, and business center to be reckoned with. There is a building off of left field that houses the "Power Pavilion" and boasts a set of bleachers on top of the building.

There are entrances mainly in the outfield and behind home plate. The concourse is a walk worth taking because you will take in every offering the stadium has with one lap. You will also notice the large amount of corporate support by Columbus companies as you walk around. This city came together to make Huntington Park happen.

In a unique layout for new ballparks, larger-than-normal concession "strands" stretch across the main concourse area behind home plate from first-base side to the third-base side. The city of Columbus is a hub to fast food and franchise family restaurants. So, it's natural that a few of the city's home restaurants (Bob Evans and Donato's Pizza) are located just outside the center-field gate. You can get barbequed beef, chicken, pulled pork, and sausages of all types at the many stands and kiosks throughout the concourse. You will not go hungry or unsatisfied at Huntington Park.

The beer selections are middle of the road to decent. You have your corporate beers combined with local labels from Columbus Brewing Company. What you will appreciate is the value fans get for food and beer selections. In a way, it is Columbus' way of saying "Yes, we aren't a big-league city and the prices prove it."

The area around the park is still in gentrification mode. This area was a state prison only a few years back. The stadium is in what locals consider the stadium district. The ballpark somewhat ties together the entertainment district for the sports and arts for Columbus. The symphony and museums of Columbus are now tied into the stadium district with the building of Huntington Park.

Tickets are affordable, food is affordable, and entertainment is nearby. Restaurants are all over this city with such a diverse economy. This may be a minor league ballpark, but it is a major league town worth a long weekend. Go to Huntington Park for the baseball and outstanding stadium, but stay in Columbus for the fun.

Dining/Bars/Nightlife
A good burger makes the **Thurman Café** (German Village, 183 Thurman Ave., Columbus) stand out. Quality American upscale can be found at the old-school **Tip Top Kitchen & Cocktails** (Downtown, 73 E. Gay St., Columbus). **Greek Street Tavern** (Upper Arlington, 3110 Kingsdale Ctr., Columbus) is becoming a place worth searching out in Columbus.

The Press Grill (741 N. High St., Columbus) is a cool, calm place to grab a cocktail and appetizer. For those looking to get their sports bar and/or pizza fix, head over to **Victory's Pizza & Grub** (543 S. High St., Columbus).

Hotels/Accommodations
Courtyard by Marriott—35 W. Spring St., Columbus, OH, 43215, (866) 925-4159
Crowne Plaza—33 E. Nationwide Blvd., Columbus, OH, 43215, (866) 925-8676

Hampton Inn—501 N. High St., Columbus, OH, 43215, (866) 767-0278
Hilton—401 N. High St., Columbus, OH, 43215, (888) 370-0980
Hyatt—350 N. High St., Columbus, OH, 43215, (866) 678-6350

 Directions

If you are coming from the north of town, you will head south on I-71 and turn onto I-670 West. Exit at Neil Avenue. Turn left at intersection onto Neil Avenue. Huntington Park's parking lot is a half a mile down the street.

If you are coming from the east or west of Columbus, you will use I-70 and exit at Fourth St. You will then continue on Fulton Street. Take a right at Front St., then a left on Nationwide Boulevard. The ballpark and parking lot will come up in less than a half a mile.

If you are coming from the south, use I-71 and exit at Front St. You will then turn left at Nationwide Boulevard. The ballpark and parking lot will come up in less than a half a mile.

Airport: Y (CMH) **Major Airlines:** Y **Car Rentals:** Y

FIFTH THIRD FIELD
HOME OF THE TOLEDO MUD HENS

AAA Affiliate of the Detroit Tigers/
International League

. . . .

406 Washington St., Toledo, OH, 43604
(419) 725-HENS / www.mudhens.com

Toledo, Ohio, is a rare American city that still has a balance of white-collar and blue-collar populations. The Toledo Mud Hens have been a cornerstone connecting the diverse population of Akron, and Fifth Third Field accommodates all.

Built in 2002, the rallying cry for the building of Fifth Third Field was the redevelopment of downtown Akron. The city wanted their existing indoor stadium (used for minor league hockey) to have a second pillar for economic development in the summer months. The natural answer was a new baseball stadium worthy to stand up to the legendary minor league history of the city.

Many of us from a certain age group learned about the Toledo Mud Hens from the 1970s television show *M*A*S*H*. Toledo native Jamie Farr played the cross-dressing corporal named Max Klinger who bucked for a Section 8 discharge so he could go home to Toledo. All Klinger could dream of was watching his beloved Toledo Mud Hens and eating Tony Packo's legendary chili dogs. The war in Korea ended and Klinger got his wish. I think Max Klinger would have liked to watch his Mud Hens at Fifth Third Field, too.

Baseball in Toledo at a minor league or semi-professional level has been around since the early 1880s. Toledo is a Detroit Tigers town and the Tigers have been associated with the Mud Hens organization off and on since the early 1930s. Toledo is close to the Michigan border. The allegiance of Toledo sports fans is mostly non-Ohio; Toledo roots more for Michigan and Notre Dame than Ohio State. Toledo roots for the Tigers and their affiliation with their parent club is a perfect match.

When you go to Fifth Third Field, you will be greeted by "Fleetwood" Walker Square. "Fleetwood" Walker was an African American ballplayer in the early 1880s for the Toledo Blue Stockings of the American Association.

Walker played 42 games in the major leagues before the unfortunate color line was drawn in baseball, which would of course last until 1947. Toledo has a great history in baseball and this plaza greets you with a heap of it.

Even though the ballpark is young in age, the history of Toledo baseball is built into Fifth Third Field. Sculptures outside of the center-field gate ("Who's Up?" by Emanuel Enriquez) and on the left-field concourse ("I Got It!" by Frank Gaylord) remind fans that baseball is still a game owned by kids and borrowed by adults. This truth is appreciated within this ballpark before you enter and get doused with more history.

The 10,000-seat ballpark is modern, roomy, and comfortable for fans. Special sections like "The Roost" exist for groups, but Fifth Third Field is mainly a wide-open ballpark for fans. Choose your seat well on crowded nights. Feel free to roam and choose on not-so-crowded nights. Fifth Third Field is intimate and much smaller than most AAA-level ballparks.

Toledo loves their food. Toledo's Fifth Third Field features many unique options to go along with a strong standard-ballpark-fare menu. If you like hot, get the Buffalo chicken wrap or bulky burrito that is a steal for the price of $5.00. Fans can grab more craft beers and specialty macro beers at Fifth Third Field than at your average ballpark. The great restaurant culture of Toledo is embraced at Fifth Third Field and you will not be short of options for great food or drink.

Tickets and parking will not break the bank, either. The top-end tickets are $12.00 and the parking will cost you $6.00 at most (if you can't find a free spot after 5:00 PM downtown). You will also feel safe in this gentrifying area of Toledo. Businesses and restaurants look out for downtown residents and visitors because they want revitalization to work for Toledo.

Ohio has had some great stadiums built for their minor league teams over the past 20 years. For a stadium that includes a great nod to a great city's baseball history, visit Fifth Third Field in Toledo.

Dining/Bars/Nightlife

When I was a kid, a Toledo-style Greek pizzeria came to town and our family gave it our undying loyalty for two decades. **Pizza Papali** (519 Monroe St., Toledo) is a real Greek pizzeria in Toledo. Give it a try and get hooked. A trip to **Tony Packo's** (1902 Front St., Toledo) is almost a requirement with a visit to Toledo and the chili dogs are pretty solid.

For burgers and a great bar grub menu, try the **Ye Olde Durty Bird** (2 S. Saint Clair St., Toledo). **The Ottawa Tavern** (1815 Adams St., Toledo) is a music venue/bar that is gaining a reputation for drawing great acts. The Black Keys were a regular act at the Ottawa Tavern on their rise to stardom.

Hotels/Accommodations

Bridge Pointe Inn—2600 Lauren Ln., Northwood, OH, 43619, (866) 925-8676

Park Inn—101 N. Summit St., Toledo, OH, 43604, (866) 767-0278

Red Roof Inn—3530 Executive Parkway, Toledo, OH, 43606, (866) 678-6350

Directions

If you are coming into Toledo from the Ohio Turnpike (I-80/I-94), take exit 64 to I-75 North. Then take I-75 North to exit 201B (Downtown). You will then turn left onto Erie St, then turn right onto Washington St.. You will see the ballpark at this point.

From the north or south, take I-75 South to exit 202A from the north or exit 201B from the south (Washington St.). The signs will lead you to the ballpark from either ramp.

From Michigan, you can take 23 South to I-475 East. From I-475 East, you will go to I-75 South. You will then take I-75 South to exit 202A (Washington St.). The signs will lead you to the ballpark from the ramp.

Airport: Y (TOL) **Major Airlines:** Y **Car Rentals:** Y

AKRON AEROS/CANAL PARK
Eastern League (AA) Affiliate of the Cleveland Indians
· ·

300 South Main Street, Akron, OH, 44308

Over the past 20 years, the level where young baseball prospects develop with stronger peer talent to prove themselves to be major league caliber is the AA level. AAA is being used more for veteran rehabilitation assignments and quick stopovers for recently drafted

college players. Akron is a perfect opportunity for Cleveland Indians fans to day trip and check out the Indians of the future.

Canal Park was built in 1997 and held affiliation with their parent club Cleveland Indians since the late 1980s. The ballpark was a perfect fit to a downtown area in need of a diversified entertainment base for their economy. Akron is lucky to have a decent corporate community who has always been supportive of the arts.

Baseball at Canal Park is athletics, but handled by the people of Akron with the same respect they would have at the opera. A ballgame at Canal Park is a respectful experience where you aren't beaten over the head with sound and can take score while concentrating on scouting some pretty good talent.

Added to this NPR-like atmosphere is a legendary minor league radio call by Jim Clark. For over 20 years, Clark has called games for the Akron Aeros with sidekick Ken Carman. A radio and listening buds are recommended. The station is WARF and their spot on the dial is 1350-AM.

What isn't very NPR-like is the food at Akron's Canal Park. The grease at Canal Park has been featured on Comedy Central's *Daily Show with Jon Stewart* and on a CNBC sports business report. The main focus of both reports was the "Three Dog Night," three encased

meats (Kielbasa, bratwurst, and hot dog) in a singular casing. This is a turducken-like monster of a combination. They have stepped it up a notch at Canal Park by creating a new dog deemed the "8th Wonder of the World Dog," which is covered with pretty much everything you have on the third shelf of your refrigerator and served to you for $8.00.

Canal Park is located in a downtown area that has many other options for entertainment, dining, and after-dinner revelry. You can keep the kids entertained in a specially designated children's area at the ballpark. Dining options are extensive and parking will not be a costly issue. The city of Akron is asking you to come downtown, spend your time, spend your money, and enjoy life in Akron.

The Akron skyline beyond the outfield wall welcomes all fans. Akron's Canal Park is a very welcoming stadium in a welcoming community. Be sure to schedule Akron into your baseball road trip through Ohio. This beautiful ballpark and community is worth a long visit.

Dining/Bars/Nightlife

Ranchero's Taqueria (286 E. Cuyahoga Falls Ave., Akron) has established itself as one of the best Mexican restaurants in Ohio. You can find a diverse offering of American favorites at **Crave** (57 E. Market St., Akron). You can get solid Italian and old-school pizza at **Luigi's Restaurant** (105 N. Main St., Akron).

Pints (426 E. Exchange St., Akron) is an "Ohio bar," meaning it serves both shots and beers and can accommodate both at a time. You can also catch up on your favorite games with no pretense in the air. For a taste of the Ohio microbrewery scene, head to the **Ohio Brewing Company** (451 S. High St., Akron). Their Tap Room features a strong menu of regular and seasonal offerings worthy of a try.

 ## Hotels/Accommodations

Country Inn & Suites—1420 Main St., Cuyahoga Falls, OH, 44221, (866) 678-6350
Holiday Inn Express—898 Arlington Ridge E., Akron, OH, 44312, (866) 573-4235
Sheraton—1989 Front St., Cuyahoga Falls, OH, 44221, (866) 767-0278

Directions

From the northeast, take I-77 South to 59 East. Take the Exchange/Cedar exit and turn right on Cedar. This will take you to Main Street. Once you turn right you will see the ballpark on the left. There are alternative routes within the city on Route 8, so advise your GPS.

From the south, take I-77 North to the Main St./Downtown exit. Follow the signs to Broadway Street. From Broadway, turn left on Exchange St., then a right on Main St., and then you will see the ballpark on the left.

From due east, take I-76 North to the Main St./Downtown exit. Follow the signs to Broadway Street. From Broadway, turn left on Exchange St., then a right on Main St., and then you will see the ballpark on the left.

From the southwest, take I-76 East to 59 East. Take the Exchange/Cedar exit and turn right on Cedar. This will take you to Main Street. Once you turn right you will see the ballpark on the left.

Airport: Y (CAK) **Major Airlines:** Y **Car Rentals:** Y

DAYTON DRAGONS/ FIFTH THIRD FIELD
Midwest League (A) Affiliate of the Cincinnati Reds
· ·
220 North Patterson Blvd., Dayton, OH, 45402

Dayton's Fifth Third Field is the second Fifth Third Field in Ohio and the third Fifth Third ballpark in the Midwest League. Road tripping through Ohio and the Midwest can get confusing and duplicitous naming doesn't help. But, Fifth Third Field in Dayton is a gem despite sharing a very familiar name.

Dayton opened the ballpark in April 2000 and hasn't looked back. In July 2011, the ballpark and organization passed up a North American record with its' 814th straight sellout. If you want to go to Fifth Third Field in Dayton, you will have to order your tickets in advance. It is not because the ballpark is especially different, it is because fans in Dayton support their team and appreciate that the talent is coming from the nearby-Cincinnati Reds of the National League.

Fifth Third Field is a very community-oriented ballpark. The organization has decided that family-friendly is very important to the baseball experience and has somewhat mastered that game. Mascots Wink and Heater the Dragons are often playing catch on the field

between innings. A superhero named Roofman monitors the roof and tosses down softer versions of the foul balls that go past the roof line to kids below. Every Dragon home run is celebrated at the scoreboard by two smoke-breathing dragons. There is no shortage of family-friendly entertainment at Fifth Third Field in Dayton.

The ballpark is big, with a massive concourse. Walks around Fifth Third Field serve dual duty: you can check out the great concession choices and help the kids come down from the energy high of seeing dragon mascots playing tricks on opposing team members.

Dayton is not that far from Cincinnati and the food is very similar to that in the Queen City. You will have your standard stadium fare like burgers and encased meats. Skyline Chili Dogs and pulled pork sandwiches with Montgomery Inn BBQ sauce are offered, too. The cheesesteak and Italian sausage stand on the first-base concourse cannot be ignored because you cannot get away from the smell. You

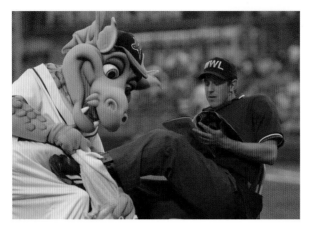

will have a higher than average amount of kid-friendly options at Dayton's Fifth Third Field, also.

Kid friendly usually means adult beverages are offered to soothe the nerves of mommy and/or daddy. The beer selection at Fifth Third Field goes above and beyond (Molson, Stella, microbrews, etc.). Parents can duck into the Fifth Third Café for a cocktail or specialty non-alcoholic drink.

Fifth Third Field is wedged into a small area of a downtown neighborhood. This is a safe area where parking will average out at $5.00. Tickets for Dragons games are a little more expensive than most Midwest League games because Dayton sells out.

I have met countless people who have been to Fifth Third Field in Dayton and none of them reported anything less than an enjoyable experience. Plan ahead and order those tickets well beforehand, though. Dayton is setting standards with Fifth Third Field. You should visit and see why.

 Dining/Bars/Nightlife

Doubleday's Grill & Tavern (199 E. Alex Bell Rd., Dayton) is home to a list of monster pizzas with monster taste. Decent pub grub can be found at **Lucky's Taproom & Eatery** (520 E. 5th St., Dayton). Upscale Chinese can be had at **C.J. Chan** (536 Wilmington Ave., Dayton).

Dayton is a university town and business center, so there are plenty of options for a drink after dinner or before the ballgame. **The Century Bar** (10 S. Jefferson St., Dayton) is a bourbon aficionado's dream. For great pizza and good beer, hit **South Park Tavern** (1301 Wayne Ave., Dayton).

 Hotels/Accommodations

Crowne Plaza—33 E. 5th St., Dayton, OH, 45402, (866) 678-6350

Dayton Grand Hotel—11 S. Ludlow, Dayton, OH, 45402, (866) 573-4235

Marriott—1414 S. Patterson Blvd., Dayton, OH, 45409, (866) 925-4159

LAKE COUNTY CAPTAINS/ CLASSIC PARK

Midwest League (A) Affiliate of the Cleveland Indians

· ·

35300 Vine St., Eastlake, OH, 44095

Classic Park is an old-style ballpark in a "beer and a shot" part of the Cleveland region whose people are as tough as nails. The people are nice, but to the point. They don't mess around. So, it only makes sense that the steel, brick, and mortar at 35300 Vine Street in Eastlake, Ohio, is nice and to the point in its design and amenities.

You will park with no hassles (which is nice). Tickets are inexpensive and readily available. The stadium signage by the ticket booth doesn't just warn people that smoking is prohibited; it states that if you are smoking in the ballpark, you are either on fire or need to go to a smoking area. Now, that is to the point.

The in-game entertainment is subdued and appropriate for a ballpark. The seats are comfortable and the stadium is easy to get around. The ballpark is reverent to the great Captains players of the past to pass through town on the way to the major leagues. The Hall of Fame in left field is helpful in guiding you through the history of the team and its effect on the area, too.

Like its fans, Classic Park's menu is blue-collar, meat and potatoes. Humphrey Bogart once said that a hot dog at the ballpark was better than a steak at the Ritz. Humphrey would love Classic Park. They keep the fare down the middle of the road and focus on the encased meats (hot dogs, brats, sausages). Fans can get Bertman's mustard at Classic Park just like they can at Progressive Field. Beer choices go from the macro-breweries to beers of the world. Some craft beer is featured at Castaway's Bar down the third-base line. But for the most part, you will not be insulted or challenged with Classic Park's menu (and that may be a good thing).

The Lake County Captains have the typical theme nights: dollar nights, and dog nights that stoke attendance upward on weekday nights. This is becoming the standard in Midwest League towns that rest on the outskirts of a Major League Baseball city. Lake County is also lucky to have the interest of the Cleveland Indians faithful in the area interested in seeing the assets of the future play within their little slice of suburbia.

The Captains mascot is named Skipper, and Skipper will entertain without harassing. The sound is not obnoxious at Lake County's Classic Field and one can reasonably do a scorecard without distraction. Most of the time, you will have a good chance to roam the stands and choose where you want to sit.

Traveling to Lake County is a bit of a throwback to a time gone by. It's nice not to have one's endorphins tested after every pitch. There is no massive sound machine or video board blaring for fear that you might fall asleep. The game is the center of attention, as it should be. You will enjoy Classic Park. It is a real place to watch real baseball with real people.

Dining/Bars/Nightlife

Eastlake locals love the carb capital that is known as **Biagio's Donut Shop & Pizzeria** (35475 Vine St., Eastlake). Biagio reportedly makes one of the best donuts in Ohio. See for yourself. Northern Ohio has had an explosion of quality Mexican restaurants and **El Palenque** (35520 Vine St., Eastlake) might be leading the charge.

The Captain's Club (34820 Vine St., Eastlake) is a distinguished dive bar down the street from the ballpark. **Trader Jack's Riverside Grille** (35901 Lake Shore Blvd., Eastlake) will get you your fix of wings, burgers, beer, and sports.

Hotels/Accommodations

Courtyard by Marriott—35103 Maplegrove Rd., Willoughby, OH, 44094, (866) 678-6350
Radisson—35000 Curtis Blvd., Eastlake, OH, 44095, (866) 573-4235
Red Roof Inn—4166 S.R. 306, Willoughby, OH, 44094, (866) 538-0251

THE FRONTIER LEAGUE

The Frontier League is a non-affiliated baseball league for college players. The teams are located in Illinois, Kentucky, Missouri, Ohio, and Pennsylvania. The Frontier League even has a traveling team (The Frontier Greys). Most players are "adopted" by local residents and live in spare rooms provided by their adopting family for the summer. Companies who support the teams often provide part-time jobs for players. Many Baseball America top 500 prospects play in the Frontier League. With some research, you can find a player or two of interest and check them out with a short side trip as part of your planned baseball road trip. Below is a list of Frontier League teams located in the state of Ohio and extreme western Pennsylvania:

Lake Erie Crushers/All-Pro Freight Stadium

2009 Baseball Blvd., Avon, OH, 44011
(440) 934-3636 / www.lakeeriecrushers.com

All-Pro Freight Stadium opened in 2009 and this beautiful stadium can seat 5,000 fans. The Frontier League stadium was recognized as the best new stadium in the area by Cleveland's *Metromix*. Special nights could hinder your ability to get tickets, so plan in advance.

Washington Wild Things (PA)*/Consol Energy Park

One Washington Federal Way, Washington, PA, 15301
(724) 250-9555 / www.washingtonwildthings.com

The uniquely designed stadium with a welcoming facade fits 3,000 and draws crowds from the Ohio, Pennsylvania, and West Virginia area. The ballpark does everything it can to keep fans attention. When the nearby Pirates are down, the Wild Things tend to draw a lot more fans. Consol Energy Park has a team store in the ballpark, a rare thing at the Frontier League level.

---

*30 miles from Ohio border

CHAPTER 9

WISSCONSIN

Beer, Brats, and Baseball

MILLER PARK

Home of the Milwaukee Brewers

· ·

1 Brewers Way, Milwaukee, WI, 53214
(414) 902-4400 / www.visitmilwaukee.com

The baseball fans of Wisconsin have so many reasons to come back to Miller Park. First, you have the most incredible tailgating in baseball. Second, you have an incredibly fun atmosphere inside the ballpark. Last, the city of Milwaukee offers fans some of the best restaurants, breweries, and neighborhoods to enjoy in a baseball town.

Milwaukee, Wisconsin, is a loyal baseball town with a heavy addiction to football. The tailgating is legendary at Green Bay Packers and Wisconsin Badgers games in Madison. It was a natural fit for Wisconsinites to adapt the practice to the parking lot at Miller Park before regular season games.

The altar at the Church of the Brewers Tailgate is the grill. The holy trinity is the bratwursts, hot dogs, and burgers. The saints are specialty items like chicken wings, pork chop sandwiches, and breakfast burritos. Cheese serves as the sacred vestments for most grilled items. The holy water is, of course, beer.

I apologize for employing sacrilege to describe something as seemingly innocuous as a tailgate at a ballgame. However, this is Milwaukee and they have taken the practice of the tailgate at a baseball game to a much higher, almost spiritual level. I highly recommend working in a tailgate on your baseball road trip to Milwaukee's Miller Park if the opportunity affords itself.

Milwaukee's Miller Park was an answer to a question that had vexed the city and county of Milwaukee since the Braves moved to Milwaukee. The Braves played in a County Stadium that had limited capacity and capability. These limitations contributed to the Braves exodus to Atlanta from Milwaukee in 1965. When the year-old Seattle Pilots went bankrupt during Spring Training of 1970, Milwaukee businessman Bud Selig organized a last-minute takeover of the Pilots franchise. The team was stranded in Provo, Utah, not knowing whether to go to Seattle or Milwaukee. In the end, the Pilots (and their colors of blue and gold) ended up in Milwaukee at what was thought to be their temporary digs of Milwaukee County Stadium.

Little did they know that "temporary" would mean 32 years. Miller Park would not become a reality until 2001. Face it: when you get a baseball franchise at the last second, things will keep you busy for a while.

No deference to those romantic about County Stadium, but it was functional at the most basic level. Opening Day bettors would handicap which second-level bathrooms pipes were frozen. Concession stands were roughed into concourses. The grandstand was hard and gray and did everything it could to look the part of professional baseball. The grandstand roof was repaired in patches and looked it from above. The bleachers were metal, uneven, and looked like they were purchased from the local high school football field. Miller Park was meant to be everything County Stadium was not.

The almost 42,000-seat Miller Park was unique for stadiums in the United States in the fact that it featured a retractable roof. Toronto's SkyDome led the charge on this front and Milwaukee wanted to make sure they learned every lesson from Toronto's experience. Milwaukee weather is Midwest weather in the fact that it can change from hour to hour without warning and sometimes with ferocity.

Miller Park mainly hosts the Brewers, but is on the ready to host just about any event. The ballpark is widely gaining a reputation as one of the best large concert venues in the Midwest. Milwaukee is among bowling's great capitals, so why not host major Professional Bowling Association events? In 2004 and 2007, the PBA set up lanes for the U.S.B.C. Masters event, drawing almost 5,000 fans per event. Thank goodness for the retractable roof.

Along with the retractable roof are sliding windows along the massive collection of windows that make up the wall behind the outfield

SIDE TRIP: BREWERY TOURS OF WISCONSIN

Wisconsin makes beer. Great beers. The state of Wisconsin has been home to breweries since well before their statehood in 1848. Americans associate this great state with brewing and beer. Fans and non-fans of beer can appreciate the brewing process up close at Wisconsin brewers, large and small by doing a brewery tour. Below is list of tours in the Milwaukee area you can try on your visit:

Historic Pabst Brewery
901 W. Juneau Ave., Milwaukee, WI, 53233
(414) 630-1609 / www.BestPlaceMilwaukee.com

Big Bay Brewing Company
4517 N. Oakland Ave, Shorewood, WI, 53211
(414) 226-6611 / www.BigBayBrewing.com

Lakefront Brewery
1872 Commerce St., Milwaukee, WI, 53212
(414) 372-8800 / www.LakefrontBrewery.com

Sprecher Brewery
701 W. Glendale Ave., Glendale, WI, 53209
(414) 964-2739 / www.SprecherBrewery.com

Milwaukee Brewing Company
613 S. Second St., Milwaukee, WI, 53204
(414) 226-2337 / www.MilwaukeeBrewingCo.com

MillerCoors
4251 W. State St., Milwaukee, WI, 53208
(414) 931-BEER or (800) 944-LITE / www.MillerCoors.com

For more information: www.milwaukeebrewerytours.com

concourse. The natural light is spectacular through this unique feature of Miller Park. The roof itself makes little if any sound when it is opened.

Miller Park is about the food. They know they have competition tailgating in the parking lot, so they take it up a level. The same goes for the beer menu: Miller Brewing and South African Breweries want to show off their products and no place is better than the hometown ballpark of the brewer.

The Brat Boys stands are located throughout Miller Park. These stands are dedicated to Wisconsin's finest meat exports: the bratwurst, Polish sausage, and Italian sausage. Klement's sausages are featured at Miller Park and the Brat Boys are pumping out thousands of them a game. When in Wisconsin, you will want to eat Klement's, Usinger's, or small butcher-shop sausages at a tailgate. Inside the stadium, you will have no difficulty finding a quality bratwurst, sausage, or hot dog.

Klement's also sponsors the sausage races. The sausage races at Miller Park are truly something every baseball fan needs to see before they die.

When it comes to food, Milwaukee is a stadium that demands a walk around the concourse previous to the game. Fans can plot out what tickles their fancy and plan which inning to get it this way. Miller Park's menu has a lot of variety, so walk the concourse and check things out before you make a commitment.

The menu isn't one that you will find at a vegan festival.

Another unusual product from Miller Park is Stadium Sauce. Stadium Sauce has a taste somewhere between a ketchup and barbeque sauce. Stadium Sauce is meant for the french fries, but fans have used it on some meat products. Mustard is king on encased meats in Milwaukee, so be careful if you are tempted to put it on a bratwurst.

Miller Park fills slowly as the game starts because of the tailgating that spills over beyond the first pitch. Wisconsinites are nice to you if you limit the up and down of getting to and leaving your seat. Code No. 1 at Miller Park is that they have beer vendors in the aisles for your convenience, so use them. Code No. 2 is that if you can't hold more than one beer at a time, you need to drink your beer on the concourse. You will be ribbed if this is the case. The Brewers fans are likely the happiest and friendliest in the game.

The Brewers fans engage with newbies to Miller Park because they are proud of the place. You will have a happy conversation with someone at Miller Park. Conversations tend to happen within sections across a few rows and always tend to be funny. Milwaukee fans understand that a day at the ballgame is much better than a day at the office. So, enjoy yourself.

Miller Park is an experience that will be enjoyed by families, groups of friends, and everyone in between. Take a long weekend and roam the great city of Milwaukee. The Milwaukee Farmer's Market downtown is stand after stand of culinary delights. Check out which summer festivals at Maier Park might appeal to you and plan a Brewers weekend around it. You will have a good time and feel welcome in Milwaukee.

Ballpark Facts, Figures, & Tips

Miller Brewing Company has a naming rights agreement for the ballpark that runs through 2020…The ballpark itself has no air conditioning, a testament to the moderate temperatures in Milwaukee…The ballpark construction started in October 1996, and was completed in early 2001…The HKS-designed stadium cost $400 million, $310 million of which was public financing…The first game played at Miller Park was a March 30, 2001, exhibition between the Chicago White Sox and Milwaukee Brewers…Former career-Brewer Robin Yount designed the layout and dimensions of Miller Park's field of play…Miller Park has a restaurant in left field (T.G.I. Friday's) that is open 360-plus days a year.

Best Tips for Seating

Every seat is a deal at Miller Park. Yearly, the Brewers and Miller Park sell tickets at a price well below the average in Major League Baseball. Fans can get behind home plate for $65.00 or even less. Great seats all over are available in the $25.00 to $40.00 range. Scalpers out front usually run a buyer's market at Miller Park. This writer got four $35.00 tickets for $5.00 per ticket for a weekday afternoon game.

Driving Directions/Transportation

From the south, northeast and east, take the I-94 westbound ramp (Madison exit), then continue on I-94 westbound to Miller Park Way.

From the northwest, take southbound 41/45 to I-94 eastbound (to Milwaukee). Follow I-94 eastbound to Miller Park Way.

From the southwest, take I-43 North to I-894 northbound. Take this to I-94 eastbound (Milwaukee). Follow I-94 eastbound to Miller Park Way.

From the west, take I-94 eastbound to Milwaukee and continue to Miller Park Way.

Many public and private shuttles exist from the downtown area. The best bus routes to Miller Park branch off of the Wisconsin Ave. route. The bus stop lets off to the south of the ballpark and is a frequent flyer toward the downtown area. To see bus routes and plan your trip, go to the Milwaukee County Transportation website at www.ridemcts.com.

Parking

You will have no problem finding parking around Milwaukee's Miller Park. There are almost 13,500 parking spaces in the immediate area of the stadium. The stadium parking spaces are larger than normal and accommodating for tailgating. These parking lots encourage tailgating. For $10.00, you and your family/group can park within a short walk of the stadium. That is, if you are early.

You can get preferred parking for an additional $5.00. Any way you cut it, Miller Park provides among the best parking in Major League Baseball.

Airport

General Mitchell International Airport (MKE)

Car Rentals

Advantage - (800) 777-5500
Alamo - (800) 327-9633
Avis - (800) 831-2847
Budget - (800) 527-0700
Dollar - (800) 800-4000
Enterprise - (800) 325-8007
Hertz - (800) 654-3131
National - (800) 328-4567

Dining/Bars/Nightlife

Milwaukee has a lot of great pizza, but among my favorite pizza places in America is **Zaffiro's Pizza** (1724 North Farwell Ave., Milwaukee). Zaffiro's cracker-thin crust and great atmosphere make it a must-experience place. **Sobelman's Pub & Grill** (1900 W. St. Paul Ave., Milwaukee) is gaining a national reputation for a great burger. If you haven't gotten your fill of German-style sausages, **Mader's Restaurant** (1041 N. Old World 3rd St., Milwaukee) serves up great German food along with a fun experience.

If you are dining on pizza at Zaffiro's, a great place for a nightcap and good time is right across the street. **Halliday's Irish Pub** (1729 N. Farwell Ave., Milwaukee). For a more sophisticated view of Milwaukee and Lake Michigan, hit **Blu** at the **Pfister Hotel** (424 E. Wisconsin Ave., Milwaukee). The view and the quality bartending are worth the prices advertised.

A few other places to consider in Milwaukee for a bite or after dinner drink:

Benji's—4156 N. Oakland Ave., Shorewood, WI, 53211 (Delicatessen)
Botanas—816 S. 5th St., Milwaukee, WI, 53204 (Mexican)
Braise—1101 S. 2nd St., Milwaukee, WI, 53204 (American)

Bartalotta's—3133 E. Newberry Blvd., Milwaukee, WI, 53211 (Italian)
La Merenda—125 E. National Ave., Milwaukee, WI, 53204 (Tapas)
Mr. Perkin's—2001 W. Atkinson Ave., Milwaukee, WI, 53209 (Soul)
Umami Moto—718 N. Milwaukee St., Milwaukee, WI, 53202 (Pan-Asian)

Hotels/Accommodations

Milwaukee's downtown area is a great place for a great time. In summer, there are few U.S. cities that match Milwaukee for fun. The festivals, events, and restaurants of Milwaukee make it a great place for a long weekend that isn't all baseball. Below are a few choices for quality hotels near Miller Park and some downtown for people looking to be in the center of the action:

Ambassador Hotel—2308 W. Wisconsin Ave., Milwaukee, WI, 53233, (866) 925-4159
Courtyard by Marriott—16865 W. Bluemound Rd., Brookfield, WI, 53005, (866) 925-8676
Days Inn—1840 N. 6th St., Milwaukee, WI, 53212, (866) 538-9298
Hilton—509 W. Wisconsin Ave., Milwaukee, WI, 53203, (866) 538-0251
Hilton Garden Inn—611 N. Broadway, Milwaukee, WI, 53202, (866) 767-0278
Hotel Metro—411 E. Mason St., Milwaukee, WI, 53202, (866) 538-6252
Marriott—323 E. Wisconsin Ave., Milwaukee, WI, 53202, (866) 925-8676
The Pfister Hotel—424 E. Wisconsin Ave., Milwaukee, WI, 53202, (866) 925-4159

Ballpark/Neighborhood Security

Miller Park is not a downtown stadium. The ballpark is actually quite west of the lakefront and downtown. Public transportation in Milwaukee is safe, but odds are you will drive to the ballpark. You will be routed into general parking and the parking lot is monitored by security. Tailgaters are friendly and keep an eye out for others as they grill and drink with revelry.

The ballpark is extremely safe. Police officers and security will willingly give any fans assistance, if needed. If you or your group plans on drinking, designate a driver. Rest up when you get back to your resting place of choice: you will want to get out and see the very safe and entertaining downtown Milwaukee.

BELOIT SNAPPERS/POHLMAN FIELD
Midwest League (A) Affiliate of the Oakland A's

2301 Skyline Drive, Beloit, WI, 53511

Beloit is a working-class town sitting on the Wisconsin border with Illinois. Recent small-scale renovations took place at the old ballpark,

but Pohlman Field still has a long way to go. Going to a Beloit Snappers game at Pohlman Field is not a day at Miller Park. There was also a change in affiliation from the Minnesota Twins to Oakland A's, which means fresh talent passing through town.

A snapper is a large turtle. The nearby Rock River in Beloit has a large number of these turtles, and thus the nickname. Pohlman Field, home of the Snappers, is not a stadium like one of throwback stadiums. It is a grandstand with a roof that provides a few obstructed views. This is a stadium with good bones. Pohlman Field has potential for a first-class renovation.

The menu at Pohlman Field is not extensive. It is recommended that you try the pulled pork sandwich. Other than that, the choices for food and drink are pretty standard and will not offend your senses. The Klement's bratwursts are a strong choice, too. You can't go wrong with a brat in Wisconsin. The beer products are Miller, with a smattering of unique labels mostly distributed by Miller/SAB.

As said before, the bones of Pohlman are strong. The stadium tries to entertain fans with family zones that include distractions for the kids and picnic tables. You don't get the overwhelming amount of "entertainment" options at Polhman Field. Truth be told, this might be welcome if you are on a baseball road trip through northern Illinois and southern Wisconsin. The Cubs, White Sox, and Brewers have constant noise filling your ears and the video board distracting your eyes. Maybe doing a scorecard and watching the game in detail is just what the doctor ordered after taking in a Major League Baseball game.

If you want a quiet Midwest League experience at a longtime Midwest League venue, try Pohlman Field. I recommend a day game as you leave the big cities of Chicago or Milwaukee. The calm may do you good.

 ### Dining/Bars/Nightlife
615 Club (615 Broad St., Beloit) is what Wisconsinites call a "supper club." Supper clubs are essentially restaurants with table cloths; a club feeling with decent food. Another choice

south of the Illinois border is **Anna Maria's Italian Restaurant** (823 Gardner St., South Beloit, IL). The South Beloit eatery offers some of the area's best pizza. For a great burger and beer combination, **Hanson's Bar** (615 Cranston Rd., Beloit).

Hotels/Accommodations
Wisconsin Timber – The Beloit Inn—500 Pleasant St., Beloit, WI, 53511, (866) 573-4235
Hampton Inn—2700 Cranston Rd., Beloit, WI, 53511, (866) 767-0278
Holiday Inn Express—2790 Milwaukee Rd., Beloit, WI, 53511, (866) 678-6350

WISCONSIN TIMBER RATTLERS/ TIME WARNER FIELD
Midwest League (A) Affiliate of the Milwaukee Brewers

2400 N. Casaloma Dr., Appleton, WI, 54912

Appleton is a city that sits in the northeastern Wisconsin shadow of football's "Titletown," Green Bay. However, Appleton's minor league baseball history goes back to almost 1890. The city of Appleton has had a continuous organization at the minor league level since 1958. The future of baseball in Appleton and the Fox Cities is strong with the 2009 affiliation agreement the Timber Rattlers made with the Milwaukee Brewers.

Throw in the fact that Appleton has made recent renovations and upgrades to Time Warner Field at Fox Cities Stadium and the future looks really bright.

Yes, technically, it is Time Warner Field at Fox Cities Stadium. However, most locals still call it Fox Cities Stadium. Time Warner Field is a by-product of a naming rights deal that doesn't affect the longtime Timber Rattlers fans. With the renovations came upgrade to the food that fans were offered at Time Warner Field. The sheer ridiculousness of the massive burgers—the spicy Venom Burger and the almost-two-pound Grand Slam Burger—offered at the ballpark are standouts on a much-improved menu at Time Warner Field. You will want to check out all of the options on the concourse because the food at

A supper club is a restaurant that the community uses as a social meeting place. In Wisconsin, supper clubs are a hub of the community. Applebee's is a restaurant, not a supper club. Supper clubs are owned by families or groups of friends who live in the community. The supper club is where you go for a great meal and a brandy after dinner with friends. You may even dress a notch better for a visit to the supper club.

There are hundreds of supper clubs across Wisconsin. Check out www. wisconsinsupperclubtour.com for a list of supper clubs wherever you are on your travels through Wisconsin.

Webster's defines a fish fry as a picnic or supper featuring fried fish. In Wisconsin, a fish fry is so much more than that simple definition. You have great fishing and great fish in Wisconsin. Specific restaurants do the fish fry very well. For the best analysis on fish frys in the town you are visiting in Wisconsin, visit www.wisconsinfishfry.blogspot.com. You really must experience quality fresh-water fish in fried form with their proper sides of cole slaw, hush puppies, and potatoes.

The state of Wisconsin consumes the most brandy per capita of any state. The unofficial state cocktail and most often consumed pre-dinner at supper clubs and better fish frys is the brandy old-fashioned sweet or "brandy sweet." A brandy sweet is three ounces of brandy, cherry juice, bitters, lemon-lime soda, a sugar cube, and garnished with a skewer of an orange slice and maraschino cherry in a highball glass with ice. Yes, it is sweet. However, it is what Wisconsinites have ramped up with before dinner for generations. Try one on your visit to a supper club to take in the full Wisconsin dining experience.

For a good website outlining the best places to take in the Wisconsin dining experience, visit www.travelwisconsin.com/dining.

Time Warner Field is above par compared to most Midwest League ballparks. This truly Northwoods ballpark offers Leinenkugel beers, a good list of alternative ales, and mixed drinks to satisfy any adult palate.

Bundle up if it isn't a summer month…including May. This area of the world is cooler and a fleece may be needed. Be aware that snakes are present at all times at Time Warner Field. Well, one snake: Fang, the Timber Rattlers mascot, is a very active mascot and will keep the kids attention. As in Milwaukee, the seventh-inning stretch is both "Take Me Out to the Ballgame" and "Roll Out the Barrel." This is still a major beer-producing state. So, grab a Leinie's, some cheese curds, and get comfortable.

Brewers fans who delve into numbers and get a better understanding of the depth of their organization's talent should make the trek to Appleton (technically, Grand Chute) for a game or two a year. Families also should consider adding a Timber Rattlers game at Time Warner Field as a Wisconsin entertainment option to rival indoor water parks and Tommy Bartlett's water skiing squirrel show. No matter how you get to Time Warner Field at Fox Cities Stadium, get there. The atmosphere, food, and drink cannot be beat in the Midwest League.

Dining/Bars/Nightlife

If you aren't watching Timber Rattlers baseball, hit the Fox Cities best Italian joint at **Carmella's** (716 N. Casaloma Dr., Appleton). Greek food is the specialty at the highly recommended **Apollon** (207 N. Appleton St., Appleton). For Japanese and sushi, **Nakashima of Japan** (4100 W. Pine St., Appleton) gets high marks.

After the game, the **Wooden Nickel Sports Bar & Grill** (217 E. College Ave.) will catch you up on your scores and serves a solid slate of beers for sports fans.

Hotels/Accommodations

Candlewood Suites—4525 W. College Ave., Appleton, WI, 54914, (866) 678-6350

Hampton Inn—350 Fox River Dr., Appleton, WI, 54913, (866) 573-4235

Super 8—3624 W. College Ave Hwy., Appleton, WI, 54914, (866) 925-4159

THE NORTHWOODS LEAGUE

The Northwoods League is a non-affiliated baseball league for college players. The teams are located in Iowa, Minnesota, Michigan, Ontario, and Wisconsin. Most players are "adopted" by local residents and live in spare rooms provided by their adopting family for the summer. Companies who support the teams often provide part-time jobs for players. Many Baseball America top 250 prospects play in the Northwoods League. With some research, you can find a player or two of interest and check them out with a short side trip as part of your planned baseball road trip. Below is a list of Northwoods League teams located in the state of Wisconsin:

Eau Claire Express/Carson Park

108 East Grand Ave., Eau Claire, WI, 54701
www.eauclaireexpress.com

This multi-use facility for the Eau Claire Parks Department has a facade for the baseball stadium made of cobbled limestone bricks. The 4,700-seat stadium also has a marble statue of former Eau Claire Bear Hank Aaron.

Green Bay Bullfrogs/Joannes Stadium

1450 E. Walnut St., Green Bay, WI, 54301
www.greenbaybullfrogs.com

The 2,000-seat ballpark in Titletown was built in 1929 and brought back to life for Northwoods League ball in 2007. The Bullfrogs organization is looking to step up the quality of the stadium over the next decade with upgrades to the facility.

Kenosha (New Franchise-2014)/Simmons Field

7817 Sheridan Rd., Kenosha, WI, 53143
www.kenoshabaseball.com

The new Northwoods League franchise in Kenosha has a historic home in Simmons Field. The ballpark was built before 1920 and was home to the Kenosha Comets of the short-lived All-American Girls Professional Baseball League featured in the movie *A League of Their Own*. Renovations are being made to Simmons Field and will be done in time for the 2014 season.

LaCrosse Loggers/Copeland Park

800 Copeland Ave., La Crosse, WI, 54603
www.lacrosseloggers.com

The 3,550-seat Copeland Park is also known as "The Lumber Yard." Recent renovations have allowed the stadium to stand among the top ballparks for attendance in the Northwoods League.

Lakeshore Chinooks/Kapco Park at Concordia University

12800 N. Lake Shore Dr., Mequon, WI, 53097
www.lacrosseloggers.com

The completely renovated 1,500-seat stadium exists as a multi-use facility for the Chinooks and nearby Concordia University. Mequon is home to a number of great golf courses and a summer farmer's market to rival those in larger cities.

Madison Mallards/Warner Park

2920 N. Sherman Ave., Madison, WI, 53704
www.madisonmallards.com

You can't help but root for the Madison Mallards. Annually, the Mallards lead the Northwoods League in attendance. The organization may also lead the league in fun, too.

"The Duck Pond" takes in crowds over 5,000 for every night game because of innovative marketing like "Curdfest" (a celebration of the Wisconsin cheese by-product/cheese nugget) and wacky Maynard Mallard entertaining kids of all ages at a break-beak pace. Owner Steve Schmitt bought the Northwoods League team in 2001 when the organization was drawing 1,000- to 2,000-fan crowds. Not only did Schmitt bring the wacky to Madison baseball fans, but also a winner.

The Mallards made the playoffs three of the first four years after Schmitt purchased the team.

Ever see a 200-pound duck fly? Well, Maynard Mallard flies into the ballpark before each game on a zip line. If the team isn't doing a promotional giveaway, they have discount tickets. To Steve Schmitt, putting butts in the seats first is the only way to get fans to buy food, drinks, and swag. So, show your appreciation by trying to make people laugh and have fun.

Watch out for foul balls. The announcer will immediately say the word "weiner." That word is code. If you get a foul ball, you win a hot dog if you turn it in.

The Mallards drew 217,143 fans in 2012. This trend has only grown each year for Madison and their ownership since 2001. For a city that lost three previous minor league franchises in the 1990s, the future looks really bright for the Mallards. Madison is a perfect overnight stop-off between Chicago and Minneapolis for any baseball road-tripping group. Enjoy and watch out for flying ducks and foul balls.

Wisconsin Woodchucks/Athletic Park

324 E. Wausau Ave., Wausau, WI, 54402
www.woodchucks.com

A $2.7 million renovation of Athletic Park will upgrade seats and common areas for fans in 2014. Luxury suites will be added as well as an improved media center. The stadium holds 3,850 fans and is comfortably shoehorned into a Wausau neighborhood. The renovation will also give continuity to the facade of Athletic Park.

Wisconsin Rapids Rafters/Witter Park

521 Lincoln St., Wisconsin Rapids, WI, 54494
www.raftersbaseball.com

Witter Park has been home to a few minor league teams in the past and the Rafters are the newest incarnation (2010). The Rafters have played in the 1,560-seat ballpark. Witter Park often gets standing-room-only crowds and maxed out at 2,415 on August 16, 2010, against Battle Creek. With attendance often maxing out beyond the seating area, Wisconsin Rapids may be pondering upgrades soon.

PHOTO CREDITS

Akron/Canal Park — David Monseur
Battle Creek/C.O. Brown Stadium — Brian Colopy
Beloit/Pohlman Field — Jim Inserra
Bowling Green/Bowling Green Ballpark — Donna Wilson
Burlington/Community Field — John Larson
Cedar Rapids/Veterans Memorial Stadium — Andrew J. Pantini
Chicago/U.S. Cellular Field and Wrigley Field — Zachary Broadwater
Cincinnati/Great American Ballpark — Shutterstock.com
Cleveland/Progressive Field — Henryk Sadura/Shutterstock.com
Clinton/Ashford University Field — Chad Seely
Columbus/Huntington Park — Ken Schnacke/Joe Santry
Dayton/Fifth Third Field — Tom Nichols
Des Moines/Principal Park — Scott Sailor
Detroit/Comerica Park — Steve Pepple/Shutterstock.com
Evansville/Bosse Field — Mike Radomski
Fort Wayne/Parkview Field — Tony DesPlaines
Gary/Southshore — Jon Mozes/Gary Southshore RailCats
Great Lakes (Midland)/Dow Diamond — Steve Livingston
Indianapolis/Victory Field — A. Murray-Bray/J. Schwab
Kane County/Fifth Third Bank Ballpark — Shawn Touney
Kansas City/Kauffman Stadium — Ffooter/Shutterstock.com
Lake County/Classic Park - Lake County Captains — Craig Deas
Lexington/Whitaker Bank Ballpark — Tyler Cobb
Louisville/Louisville Slugger Field — Louisville Bats
Madison/Warner Park — Katie Richard
Milwaukee/Miller Park — Action Sports Photography / Shutterstock.com
Minneapolis/Target Field — Natchapon L./Shutterstock.com
Peoria/Dozer Park — Dennis Sievers
Quad Cities/Modern Woodmen Ballpark — Sean Flynn
Schaumburg/Boomers Stadium — Kyle Hampson
South Bend/Coveleski Stadium — Joe Hart
St. Louis/Busch Stadium — Daniel M. Silva/Shutterstock.com
St. Paul/Midway Stadium — Emily Robertson
Toledo/Fifth Third Field — Toledo Mud Hens Baseball Corp.
West Michigan (Grand Rapids)/Fifth Third Ballpark — Mickey Graham
Whiting/Oil City Stadium — NWI Baseball LLC/Northwest Indiana Oilmen
Wisconsin Timber Rattlers/Time Warner Field — Ann Mollica